Skills in ENGLISH

1

Lindsay McNab
Imelda Pilgrim
Marian Slee

Heinemann

Published by Heinemann Educational Publishers
Halley Court, Jordan Hill, Oxford OX2 8EJ
A division of Reed Educational and Professional Publishing Ltd

OXFORD MELBOURNE AUCKLAND
JOHANNESBURG BLANTYRE GABORONE
IBADAN PORTSMOUTH NH (USA) CHICAGO

First published 2000
2004 2003 2002 2001 2000
10 9 8 7 6 5 4 3 2

ISBN 0 435 19322 8

Illustrations
Original illustrations © Heinemann Educational Publishers 2000

Illustrations
Rosalind Hudson: page 19, 20; Andrew Quelch: page 16, 17, 40, 41, 54, 172; Sarah Warburton: page 34, 86, 99, 101, 135; Nick Duffy: page 30, 66, 83, 109, 111, 130, 133, 155; Chris Long: page 7, 47, 98, 115; Alice Englander: page 13, 14, 112; Carey Bennett: page 22, 23, 51, 136; Tim Davies: page 64, 77, 126, 145, 177; Nick Schon: page 8, 27, 67, 105, 141, 161, 165, 188; Rosie Woods: pages 10, 11, 42; DTP Gecko: pages 25, 53, 117, 157, 158; Julian Mosedale: page s 28, 29, 44, 110, 174; Kiran Ahmad: pages 60; Tim Etheridge: pages 163; Joanne Moss: pages 81, 94; Abigail Conway: pages 82, 90, 149; Louise Morgan: page 87; Nadime Faye-James: pages 106, 107; Martin Sanders: page 152; Chris Long: page 159, 173, 187

Designed by 320 Design. Produced by Gecko Ltd, Bicester, Oxon
Printed and bound in Spain by Mateu Cromo

Copyright permissions sought by Jackie Newman

Photo research by Jennifer Johnson

Tel: 01865 888058 www.heinemann.co.uk

Introduction

WORDS ARE ALL AROUND US – written down for us to read and spoken for us to listen to. We have so many words in our heads – words to write down, to be read by others, and words to speak, to be listened to by others.

The study of English is about the study of words and how they are placed together. It is a study that starts when we are born and first hear the rhythms of the words spoken to us. It is a study that continues throughout our lives as we gain an ever increasing range of words and an awareness of the effects they can have. Understanding words and how they are used allows us to better understand other peoples' ideas and to communicate our ideas to them.

Through this book, and the CD-ROM that accompanies it, you will find out a lot more about words. You will develop your skills in reading, writing and speaking and listening. You will read the words of other writers, and be helped to understand their meanings and appreciate their skills. You will write your own words and be guided in your choice of the best words to use and shown how to make the most of them. You will be involved in a range of speaking and listening activities and be advised on how to make sure your words count.

We hope you enjoy the texts and the activities that we have chosen for you and that, through them, you will develop your skills in English.

CONTENTS

The publishers gratefully acknowledge the following for permission to reproduce copyright material. Every effort has been made to trace copyright holders, but in some cases it has proved impossible. The publishers would be happy to hear from any copyright holder that has not been acknowledged.

Extract adapted from 'The Seven Pomegranate Seeds' taken from ***Myths and Legends*** by Anthony Horowitz, published by Kingfisher and reprinted by permission of The Maggie Noach Literary Agency Limited, p10; extract adapted from 'The Grendel' taken from ***Myths and Legends*** by Anthony Horowitz, published by Kingfisher and reprinted by permission of The Maggie Noach Literary Agency Limited, pp12-15; extract adapted from 'Catching the Sun' taken from ***Myths and Legends*** by by Anthony Horowitz, published by Kingfisher and reprinted by permission of The Maggie Noach Literary Agency Limited, pp16-17; extracts from 'Le Morte D Arthur', by Thomas Malory, edited and abridged by Helen Cooper (Oxford Worlds Classics 1998), reprinted by permission of Oxford University Press, pp19-20 ; 'It is Night' by Janice E. Parkin, originally published in T.A.S.C. Poetry, p22; 'The Washing Machine' by Jeffrey Davies, taken from Wordspinners published by OUP, used with the kind permission of Mrs. S. Davies, p22; 'One' by James Berry, taken from ***When I Dance*** published by Puffin, © 1998 James Berry, reprinted by permission of The Peters Fraser and Dunlop Group Limited on behalf of James Berry, p23; 'Superstink' by Robert Froman, used with the kind permission of Mrs Froman, p25; 'Revolver' by Allan Riddell, reprinted by permission of Calder Trust, London, p25; 'Obstacles' by Lorraine Simeon, reprinted by permission of the author, p26; 'At the Match - Harry's Monologue' by Peter Terson, reproduced by permission of The Agency (London) Limited, first published in ***Zigger Zagger*** by Penguin Books © Peter Terson, all rights reserved and enquiries to: The Agency (London) Limited, p27; 'U.S. Flies in Hamburgers' by Roger McGough, © Roger McGough, reprinted by permission of Peters Fraser and Dunlop Limited on behalf of Roger McGough, p28; 'The Fly' by Walter de la Mare, reprinted by permission of The Literary Trustees of Walter de la Mare, and the Society of Authors as their representatives, p30; extract from ***The Sword in the Stone*** by T.H. White, published by HarperCollins Publishers Limited, used with permission of the Publisher, pp32-33; extract from ***Buddy*** by Nigel Hinton, reproduced with permission of Curtis Brown Ltd., London, on behalf of Nigel Hinton, © Nigel Hinton 1982, p34; extract from ***The Witches*** by Roald Dahl, published by Penguin Books, reprinted by permission of David Higham Associates Limited, pp37-38; illustration from ***The Witches*** by Roald Dahl, illustrated by Quentin Blake published by Johnathan Cape, reproduced by permission of Random House Group Limited on behalf of Quentin Blake p37; extract from ***Blue Remembered Hills*** by Dennis Potter, first published in 1984 as ***Waiting for the Boat*** published by Faber and Faber Limited, © Dennis Potter 1984, 1996, reprinted by permission of Judy Daish Associates Limited, p39; extracts from ***Harry Potter & the Philosopher's Stone*** by J.K. Rowling, © J.K. Rowling 1997, reprinted by permission of Christopher Little Literary Agency, pp40, 41 and 96-97; extracts from ***Rice Without Rain*** by Minfong Ho, first published in 1986 by Andre Deutsch Limited, © Minfong Ho 1986, reprinted by permission of Scholastic Limited, pp42-43; extract from ***Street Child*** by Berlie Doherty, published by HarperCollins Publishers Limited, reproduced with permission of the Publisher, pp44-46; 'Chinese Puzzle Over William the Fish' reproduced by permission of Wessex News Agency, p48; 'Wild At Heart' logo, reprinted by permission of Cutting Edge, p48; Swimming-pool timetable taken from Hambleton Leisure Centre leaflet, reprinted by permission of Hambleton District Council, p48; extract from NSPCC letter, reprinted by permission of the NSPCC, p49; 'Bear's Breakfast Recipe' taken from ***The Teddy Bear Cookbook***, © Octopus Books Limited 1986, first published by Dean, an imprint of Egmont Children's Books Limited, London and used with permission, p49; ***Exploring Home Economics Bk1*** by Ruth Riddell, Lorraine Scott and Lynn Rogers, 2nd edition, 1988 Addison Wesley Longman Australia, used with permission, p51; extract and photos from ***Worldview 1*** by Fred Martin and Audbrey Whittle, reprinted by permission of Heinemann Educational, p52; extract from ***See Through History - The Vikings*** by Anne Pearson, reprinted by permission of Heinemann Educational, p55; Jelly Belly leaflet, reprinted by permission of Herman Goelitz Inc., Fairfield, CA 94533-6741, USA, p56; York Dungeons leaflet reproduced with permission of Merlin Entertainments Group, p56; Scarborough Sea-Life Centre leaflet reproduced with permission of Merlin Entertainments Group, p57; Birds of Prey leaflet reproduced with permission of Falconry UK Ltd., p58; page from Leeds United Football Club website, reproduced by permission, p59; Pass the Bomb instructions, reproduced by permission of H.P. Gibson & Sons Ltd., p62; advert for Sheehan's Music Services, reproduced with permission of Sheehan's Music Services, p63; index from ***Usborne World of the Unknown*** reproduced from ***World of the Unknown UFOs*** by permission of Usborne Publishing, © 1989, 1977 Usborne Publishing Limited, p68; extracts reproduced from ***Alien Abduction*** by permission of Usborne Publishing, © 1997 Usborne Publishing Limited, p69; extracts reproduced from ***Hotshots - UFOs*** by permission of Usborne Publishing, © 1996, 1995, 1992, 1977 Usborne Publishing Limited, pp71-74; extract 'The Man Who Took on Jaws... And Survived' from ***Today Newspaper*** 14.6.95, © News International, used with permission, pp75-76; postcard of Mallorca, reprinted with permission of Fisa - Escudo de Oro SA, Barcelona, p80; extract from ***Tuck Everlasting*** by Natalie Babbitt © Natalie Babbitt 1975, reprinted by permission of Farrar, Straus and Giroux LLC, p81; text from ***Dark, Dark Tale*** by Ruth Brown, reprinted by permission of Anderson Press, p82; extracts from ***Skellig*** by David Almond published by Hodder and Stoughton Publishers, © 1998 David Almond, reproduced by permission of Hodder and Stoughton Limited, pp84, 90 and 169; extract from ***Granny Was a Buffer Girl*** by Berlie Doherty, © 1986 Berlie Doherty, published by Methuen Children's Books and Mammoth, imprints of Egmont Children's Books Limited, London, and used with permission, p87; extract from ***Woman in Black*** by Susan Hill, published by Vintage, © Susan Hill 1983, reprinted by permission of Sheil Land Associates Limited, p88; extract from ***Someone Like You*** by Roald Dahl, published by Penguin Books, reprinted by permission of David Higham Associates Limited, p88; 'The Green Thing' from ***Monsters*** by Richard Haycroft and Nicholas Luxmore, published by Hodder & Stoughton Educational, reprinted by permission of the Publisher, p89; extract from ***Left in the Dark*** by John Gordon, reprinted by permission of A.P. Watt Limited on behalf of John Gordon, p92; extract from ***Goodnight Mr Tom*** by Michelle Magorian (first published by Penguin Books 1981), © Michelle Magorian, reproduced by permission of the author c/o Rogers Coleridge and White Ltd., p94; extract from ***I Found This Shirt: Poems & Prose From The Centre*** by Ian McMillan, published by Carcanet Press Limited, reproduced by permission of Carcanet Press Limited, p98; extract from ***How Green You Are!*** by Berlie Doherty, published by Macmillan Education, © Berlie Doherty, reprinted by permission of David Higham Associates Limited, p100; extract from ***Burning Everest*** by Adrian Flynn, first published in Heinemann Play Series, reprinted by permission of the author, pp102-104; 'The Sound Collector' by Roger McGough, from ***You Tell Me*** published by Viking Kestrel, © Roger McGough, reprinted by permission of Peters Fraser and Dunlop Group Limited on behalf of Roger McGough, p109; 'Alligator' by Spike Milligan reproduced by permission of Spike Milligan Productions Ltd., p110; extract from the poem 'Octopus or Octopuss' by Stewart Henderson, © 1994 used with the author's permission, first published in the anthology ***READ ME*** published by Macmillan 1998, p111; extract from 'Cleaning Ladies' by Kit Wright, reprinted by permission of the author, p111; extract from 'Fireworks' by James Reeves, taken from ***Complete Poems for Children*** published by Heinemann, © James Reeves, reprinted by permission of the James Reeves Estate, p111; extract from 'On Roofs of Terry Street' by Douglas Dunn, taken from ***Terry Street*** by Douglas Dunn, published by Faber and Faber Limited, reprinted by permission of Faber and Faber Limited, p111; extract from 'The Butcher' by Craig Raine, taken from the ***Onion Memory*** © Craig Raine 1978, reprinted with permission, p111; extract from 'Baldanders' by Christopher Reid, reproduced by permission of the author, p111; 'A Simile Riddle' by Stanley Cook, reprinted by permission of Mrs. S. Matthews, p113; TV listings (BBC1) taken from TVTimes 17th August 1999, reproduced with kind permission of TVTimes and the BBC, p116; extract from ***Second World War*** by Nigel Kelly, reprinted by permission of Heinemann Educational, p117; 'Swimming Fish Cakes' taken from ***Show Me How: I Can Cook***, published by Anness Publishing Ltd., reproduced with permission of Anness Publishing Limited, P119; advert for Bobby Roberts Super Circus, used with permission, p119; 'Teeth's Little Hereos' from the National Dairy Council leaflet ***Enjoy Your Food - Flight DK***, reproduced by kind permission of the National Dairy Council, p119; extract 'Wheels: Focus on this' by Miranda Sawyer, first published in ***The Observer Magazine*** 28.11.99 photos by Matt Cooke, used with permission, p120; instructions from Scaredy Cat, reproduced by permission of Orchard Toys, p134; Blackpool Sea-Life Centre map reproduced by permission of Merlin Entertainments Group, p137; Camelot Theme Park leaflet, reproduced by permission of Camelot Theme Park, pp138-139; 'Conversation Piece' by Gareth Owen, first published in ***Salford Road and Other Poems*** published by Young Lions, © 1988 Gareth Owen, reproduced by permission of the author c/o Rogers Coleridge and White Limited, p147; extract from ***Iron Woman*** by Ted Hughes, published by Faber and Faber Limited, reproduced by permission of Faber and Faber Limited, p148; extract from ***The Art of Folding Paper*** by Robert Harbin, © 1968 Robert Harbin, first published by Hodder Paperbacks Limited, reprinted by permission of The British Origami Society and Rupert Crew Ltd., pp157-158; extract 'Sophie's Mum' taken from ***Manchester Evening News*** 8.3.99, reproduced by permission of Guardian Media Group Plc., p165; extract from Dennis the Menace © D.C. Thomson & Co. Ltd., originally published in ***The Beano***, reproduced by permission of D.C. Thomson & Co. Ltd., p175; extract 'Real Life Bugs', taken from ***Funday Times*** - 14.2.99, © Times Newspaper 1999, used with permission, p179; extract from ***The Growing Pains of Adrian Mole*** by Sue Townsend, published by The Random House Publishing Group, used with permission of Random House UK Limited, p181; extract from ***My Year*** by Roald Dahl, published by Jonathan Cape, reprinted by permission of David Higham Associates Limited, p182; extract from ***Mrs Frisby and Rats and Nimh*** by Robert C. O'Brien (Victor Gollancz/Hamish Hamilton 1972), © Robet C. O'Brien 1971 used with permission of Penguin Books Limited, p183.

The publishers would like to thank the following for permission to reproduce photographs on the pages noted:

FLPA/J. Zimmermann, p61; FLPA/John Tinning, p67; Photodisc, p69; Photodisc, p71; Photodisc, p74; Collections/Dorothy Burrows, p85 (top left); Format/Melanie Friend, p85 (top right); FLPA/Derek Middleton, p85 (bottom left); Collections/Fay Godwin, p 85 (bottom right); Photodisc, p108; FLPA/S. McCutcheon, p113; J. Alan Cash Ltd., p128; Collections/Lesley Howling, p151.1; Collections/Brian Shuel, p151.2; Sally & Richard Greenhill, p151.3; Collections/Lesley Howling, p151.4; Collections/Anthea Sieveking, p151.5; Sally & Richard Greenhill, p151.6; Sally & Richard Greenhill, p151.7; Sally & Richard Greenhill, p151.8; Collections/Brian Shuel, p151.9; Collections/Paul Bryans, p151.10; Gareth Boden, p151.11; Gareth Boden, p151.12; Photodisc, p162 all photos; FLPA/L. Lee Rue, p168; Photodisc, p170 both photos; Photodisc, p171; Photodisc, p172; Collections/Brian Shuel, p178; FLPA/D. Maslowski, p179.

Section A ◆ Reading Introduction

You probably started to learn to read when you were quite young. At first you would have read from very simple books, which had lots of pictures in them and just a few words on each page. Without realising it, you were already forming an attitude towards reading.
This attitude will have been influenced by different things, including:

- how successful you were in learning to read
- whether you were encouraged to read at home
- the skill and enthusiasm of your teachers.

Reading is to the mind what exercise is to the body.
SIR RICHARD STEELE
1672–1729

You are at secondary school now and can probably read most of the words on a page. There may be some you still struggle with, but if you take your time you can usually work out how to say them. If you use a dictionary, you can find out what they mean and you will probably recognise them next time. Think back to your first days at primary school and you will see just how much progress you have made with your reading.

Now that you have the basic skills in reading, you are ready to move on. Reading is much more than simply being able to translate the letters on the page into words. It is about understanding the thoughts and ideas of another person, and about entering different imaginary and real worlds.

In this book you will find many different types of reading texts. The exercises that accompany them will help you to develop your skills in reading. But don't stop there. Once you know what kind of things you like to read, go to your library, the Internet, your newsagent or local bookshop. Find the things you want to read. Find the things that make you think. And finally, find the time to learn from them and to enjoy them.

A1 Reading literature

The word literature has a number of different meanings. In this book it is used to describe the range of written material that is linked with the imagination and making things up. This includes prose, which may be short stories or novels, poetry and play scripts. In this section the focus is mainly on the reading of stories and poetry. You will find out more about play scripts in the *Different voices* unit on page 93.

There are three units of work in this section:

The first unit, *Understanding stories from long ago*, looks at stories that are part of our heritage. It will help you to understand how a story is constructed and to identify the features that help to make a good story.

The second unit, *Ways into poetry*, will introduce you to a range of poetic forms and give you a greater understanding of the techniques that poets use.

The third unit, *Thinking about people and places*, looks closely at the techniques writers use in order to write descriptively. You will learn about the importance of choosing words carefully and will become more aware of the effects that words can have.

At the end of the section there is an assignment which tests you on the skills you will develop by working carefully through the three units.

1 Understanding stories from long ago

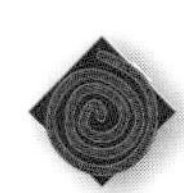

This unit will help you to:
- read for meaning
- pick out key points and stages in a story
- recognise familiar features of a story
- refer to the text when answering questions
- develop an awareness of changes in language over time.

Thinking about stories

Have you ever wondered what makes writers want to write?
Do you think they want to:
- pass on knowledge
- explain an idea
- entertain their readers?

Perhaps it is a mixture of all these things and more.
What other reasons can you think of?

There are millions of books in our world, and millions of writers, both past and present. Most people who write do so because they have ideas that they want to communicate to others.

But what happened before there were books? How did people express their ideas when they had no pens, no paper and no written language?

The answer is that they told stories.

Before there were books, and for many years after, storytelling was an important way of passing on knowledge and beliefs. Often the stories took the form of **myths**, an English term which comes from the Greek word *mythos* meaning *word*, *saying* or *story*.

Across the world, peoples of the past told stories. Sometimes these stories were about powerful gods and goddesses who governed the lives of humans. In telling them, people would often use their imagination to try to solve the mysteries of life and nature. The following story comes from Ancient Greece. It tries to explain something about the natural world, in a way that was understandable to the people of that time.

The Abduction of Persephone

The goddess Demeter protected the crops and soil for mankind. She had a beautiful daughter called Persephone, whom she loved more than anything in the whole world. Persephone's father was Zeus, the ruler of all the gods. Zeus had a brother called Hades who was the god of the Underworld. He 5 had fallen in love with Persephone and wanted to take her to his dark and dismal kingdom. Knowing that he would never get Zeus' permission for this, he kidnapped her one day while she was out picking flowers with some friends.

When Demeter learned of what had happened she was desperate with grief 10 and went to Zeus for help. Zeus explained that if Persephone had eaten so much as a mouthful of food in his brother's kingdom of the dead she would be forced to remain in the Underworld for ever. He did not want to start an argument with his brother and refused to do anything. In fury, Demeter said that she would no longer protect the earth and that it would be a barren 15 place until her daughter was returned safely.

Throughout the following year there was a terrible famine on earth. All the crops died and the trees yielded no fruit. Zeus was very concerned for mankind and so sent his messenger Hermes to plead with Hades for Persephone's return. Hades pretended to agree with what Hermes said, but 20 all the time he knew that Persephone had secretly eaten seven pomegranate seeds and that, because of this, she could not return to the world of the living.

When Zeus heard of this he held a conference to discuss what should be done. It was decided that Persephone's time should be shared between the 25 two worlds; she would spend nine months of the year with her mother and the other three months with Hades in the Underworld.

And so it is that for three months every year, the cold season comes and it looks as though the world has gone into mourning. Then the trees lose their leaves and nothing will grow until the spring, when Persephone is 30 released from the darkness of the Underworld and her mother celebrates her return.

Word bank

abduction – kidnapping

Activity 1

1 How well have you understood what is happening in the story? Answer the following questions:

- **a** Who was the goddess Demeter?
- **b** Who were Persephone's parents?
- **c** Who kidnapped Persephone, and why?
- **d** What did Zeus explain to Demeter?
- **e** What action did Demeter take?
- **f** Which messenger did Zeus send to Hades?
- **g** Why was Persephone unable to return to the world of the living?
- **h** What agreement was finally made?

2 Remember that the story was written to explain something about the natural world. What is it that this story tries to explain? Do you think it is a good explanation? Give reasons for your answer.

3 Can you think of any other stories that were once told to explain things that people could not understand? Make a list of them and say what they try to explain.

The peoples of the past did not tell stories only to explain the world around them. Just like today, they wanted to excite and entertain their listeners. When we look at stories of the past, we find many of the qualities that still make a good story today. Read the following extract based on the old English **epic** poem *Beowulf*:

Beowulf

There was a time when the court of King Hrothgar of Denmark rang with music and laughter. The great banqueting hall, Heorot, was the home of feasting and singing and of storytelling. All that was to change on the night our story begins ...

5 The Grendel heard the music of the harps ringing out across the fields. Curled up in the darkness of the swamp, the Grendel heard and one poisoned eye flickered open. Softly it growled to itself. For the Grendel understood nothing of pleasure and so hated it. Hatred ruled its life. The bitterness of centuries ran in its veins, **congealing** its blood. In its every waking moment it 10 writhed in a torment of self-pity and half-formed dreams of revenge. Now, hearing the sound, it slithered through the mud and began to limp towards the hall.

It was at that grey time between night and day when it reached Heorot. Now, at last, the revellers were asleep, intoxicated by wine and good 15 companionship. The Grendel struck quickly and greedily. Thirty warriors were snatched up from where they lay. Thirty brave men met a brutal, cowardly death. Glutted with blood, the Grendel slunk away, back to the solitude of the swamp. Even in its victory, it knew no pleasure. It had done what it had set out to do: neither more nor less.

20 Twice more the Grendel came to Heorot, each time returning in the twilight hours to claim another thirty Danish warriors. After that, the hall was closed.

A shadow had fallen across the whole country. Sometimes, in sadness, King Hrothgar, who was now an old man, would return to his beloved Heorot and sit in the silence with only his memories to keep him company. It was there, 25 some twelve years later, that he met Beowulf.

The king was sitting in his chair when the door of the banqueting hall crashed open. He squinted as bright sunlight flooded in, capturing a million **motes** of dust within its golden beams. A figure stepped forward, silhouetted against the light which could almost have been **emanating** from his own body. 30 The dust formed a shimmering **aura** around him. The king trembled. Never had there been a warrior so tall, so strong.

The stranger approached and fell onto one knee. He was dressed in a blue cloak over a silvery mail shirt. In one hand he carried a richly-decorated shield, in the other a spear. His helmet masked his face, but it could not hide

35 the fair hair that tumbled down onto his shoulders, nor the bright blue eyes that shone despite the shadows.

'Your majesty!' the figure said. 'My name is Beowulf. I have crossed a great sea to come
40 before you, to serve you and to destroy the monster that brings such terror to your land.'

Word bank

congealing – thickening
motes – specks
emanating – coming
aura – halo

As we are reading stories, we often make guesses about what will happen next. Often these guesses are based on stories we already know and on clues given to us by the writer. Sometimes we make correct guesses and sometimes there is an unusual twist in the story that we didn't expect. Before you read on, try to predict what will happen in this story and why you think this. Write down your prediction and explanation so that you can look back at it later.

The king welcomed Beowulf and that night, for the first time in many years, the floors of Heorot were swept, the tables cleaned and the beacons and fires relit. That night, as the Danes feasted and sang, the echoes of their voices were 45 carried by the wind out over the swamp. Slowly they drifted until, as the fires of Heorot were dampened and sleep replaced laughter, they reached the lair of the Grendel. Once again, the poisonous yellow eyes flickered open. Once again, reaching out with one hand, it pulled itself to its feet.

Gliding through the shadows, the Grendel came. Pushing through the mists that 50 shrouded the moors, it pressed on towards Heorot. When at last it saw the hall, its pace quickened. One scaly foot came down on a twig, snapping it. Beowulf heard the sound and opened his eyes.

The Grendel reached the door of Heorot.

At the touch of its hands, the solid wood crumpled like paper. Two 55 flames ignited in its eyes as it stepped inside. Saliva dripped from its mouth.

Beowulf had expected it to make straight for him. But one of the young soldiers had chosen to sleep on the other side of the door, and it was this unfortunate youth that the monster seized first, tearing him into pieces and swallowing them whole.

60 Only then, driven to a brutal frenzy by the taste of blood, did the Grendel stretch out its hands and seize Beowulf.

At once it knew that it had made a fatal mistake. Even as its claws tightened, it found itself grasped with a strength that it would have thought impossible in a human. Suddenly afraid, it tried to 65 pull away, to slither back into the darkness in which it had been born, but it was too late. Its whole arm was frozen in Beowulf's grip. Struggle though it might, it could not escape.

The Grendel screamed at Beowulf, their heads so close that they almost touched. The monster which had never once in its 70 life known fear had now discovered terror. It had to get away, away from the impossible man who still held it in a savage grip. And away it went – snapping the tendons in its own shoulder, unlocking the bones and tearing the skin. Howling with pain, it fled from Heorot, back into the night, blood gushing 75 from the horrible wound that it had inflicted on itself.

Word bank

ignited – caught fire
tendons – bands of tissue attaching muscles to bones

And inside the hall, Beowulf held the dreadful trophy of his victory. It was the monster's hand, its arm, its entire torn-off shoulder. These he hung beneath the gable of the roof. Heorot was cleansed. Never again would the creature return.

80 For the Grendel was dying. Even as it fled, sobbing through the night, its life-blood was flowing out of it. By the time it reached its home in the swamp, it was cold, colder than it had ever been before. Tears flowed from its eyes as it buried its raw jagged shoulder in the mud, trying to ease the pain.

85 When dawn finally came, it was dead. It had died miserably, alone in its lair, and its soul had been welcomed in Hell.

Activity 2 WS ICT

Talk about questions 1–4 and write your answer to question 5.

1. Look back at your prediction. Were you right? Look back at the features of the first part of the story that may have helped you to predict correctly what would happen.
   - The story has a monster.
   - The monster has been terrorising a country.
   - The king has grown old and sad.
   - A hero has arrived.
   - He promises to help the king and destroy the monster.

   Can you name any other stories that are based on similar ideas? You may have read them in books or seen them on TV or film. How do they usually end?
2. Look at the way the Grendel is described in lines 5–12. How does the writer create an impression of evil? Look at the description of Beowulf in lines 30–37. How does the writer make him seem good?
3. The second part of the story tells you about the fight between the hero, Beowulf, who represents good, and the monster, the Grendel, who represents evil. Can you name any other stories in which a fight between good and evil takes place? Which one usually wins?
4. Think about the fight itself, which forms the climax of the story. The monster meets a grisly end, losing its arm and bleeding to death. Can you name other stories in which there is a lot of bloodshed? Why are stories like this so popular?
5. In what ways is the ancient story of the Grendel and Beowulf similar to any present-day stories that you know?

As stories are told and retold through the ages, they change. The teller may add bits or leave bits out or take a different view of the events in the story. The following story is based on a Polynesian myth. Like the story of Persephone on page 10, it tries to explain something about the natural world. In this case the central figure is a human not a god, though he does still have magical powers. He is not, however, a hero like Beowulf, because he is something of a comedian. As you are reading, decide what you think the story is trying to explain about the natural world.

Catching the Sun

To look at, you would not have thought that Maui was a hero. He was very small and very ugly with short, stubby arms and a pot belly. And yet, to the Polynesian people, Maui was one of the greatest of the so-called trickster heroes – which is to say that what he lacked in dignity and grace he made up for in cunning. Maui had a magic jawbone given to him by an ancestor. In his lifetime he had many adventures, but perhaps his most extraordinary feat was the catching of the sun.

The adventure began one evening, just as the sun was setting. He and his four brothers had been out fishing but now, as the darkness set in, they were forced to return home. In those days, of course, there was no electricity or gas. The day ended once it got dark.

'If only the sun stayed up longer,' Maui said, 'we'd all be better off.'

The words were no sooner out of his mouth than he was struck by a thought.

'Hey!' he cried. 'Why don't we catch it?'

His brothers looked at him wearily.

'We couldn't,' one said. 'It's too far away.'

'And too big,' added a second.

'And even if we did catch it,' a third muttered, 'it would only burn us up.'

'It's impossible,' the fourth agreed.

'Nonsense!' Maui shouted. 'Of course we can do it!'

For the next week, the five brothers worked, spinning and twisting ropes to form the noose with which they would catch the sun. At last, when the noose was ready, they set off. They travelled only at night so that the sun, hidden beneath the horizon, would not see them coming. By day they hid in the desert, sleeping under bushes or covering themselves with a layer of sand. For several months they travelled until finally they arrived at the very eastern edge of the world.

Here, working under Maui's supervision, they built an
35 enormous clay wall with two sheds – one at each end. The sheds were for Maui's brothers to hide in so that they would not get burnt by the sun. The noose was unpacked and dangled over the wall so that it hung in outer space – just underneath the world itself. Maui took his place, standing at
40 the very centre of the world.

And thus prepared, they waited.

Dawn arrived and the unsuspecting sun began its climb.

'It's coming,' Maui whispered, the light dancing in his eyes.

His brothers, hidden in their sheds, tightened their grips
45 on the ends of the ropes.

The sun drew level with the wall.

'Now!' Maui cried, and slipped the noose over it.

At once the sun tried to back away. Brilliant flames exploded around it, tearing at the dark blue fabric of the
50 universe. Had Maui been an ordinary human, he would have been frazzled. But as the furious heat of the sun raced through him, he just laughed and pulled at the rope.

The noose tightened. The sun was caught.

'Now I'll teach you, you old rascal!' Maui giggled and,
55 lifting his magic jawbone, he walloped the sun half a dozen times.

'Aaagh!' screamed the sun.

Again and again Maui pounded the sun with the jawbone, sparks flying every time it made contact.

60 'Stop it!' the sun yelled. 'What have I done to you?'

But Maui was beside himself with excitement and didn't stop until, at last, he tired of the sport. Climbing back down from the wall, he signalled to his brothers who allowed the noose to open again. The sun slipped out and continued its
65 upward climb.

But it was not the same sun that had once circled the earth in seven and a half hours. Now it was bruised, battered and bewildered, quite exhausted by the clobbering it had received at Maui's hands. From that day on, it took twenty-
70 four hours to make the round trip – twelve hours from horizon to horizon. Maui had not only caught the sun. He'd beaten the living daylights out of it too!

What does this story try to explain about the natural world?

Activity 3 WS

You are going to look at the way a story can change depending on who is telling it. This story of Maui is told by a **narrator**. You are going to think about how it would change if it were told by Maui.

Task: Imagine you are Maui. Write your explanation of how you caught the sun.

In order to complete this task, you need to decide which key points Maui would include and how he would tell the story.

1 The key points are the main things that happen in the story. Make a list of them. The first four are done for you:

- Maui decided to catch the sun because he wanted more daylight.
- His brothers thought it was impossible.
- The five brothers made a noose with which to catch the sun.
- They travelled, by night, to the eastern edge of the world.

Complete the list of key points.

2 Now think about Maui. What kind of person is he? Which of the following words would you use to describe him?

◆ brave ◆ proud ◆ big-headed ◆ mischievous ◆ imaginative ◆ bossy ◆ shy

Put your words in a chart like the one below and support your choices with evidence from the story.

Words	Reason for choice
brave	*Maui is prepared to try and catch the sun even though his brothers think it can't be done.*

Can you think of any other words to describe Maui? Add them to your chart and explain why you have chosen them.

What difference would the kind of person Maui is make to the way he tells the story?

3 You are now ready to do the task. Re-read the instructions. Remember, you are to tell the story as though you are Maui.

You could start your story with this sentence:

One day I was out fishing with my brothers and I was cross that we had to go home so early because it had got dark.

4 Now re-read the original story and your own version of it. In what ways are they

a) similar?

b) different?

One story that has been retold many times and by many different people is the **legend** of King Arthur and the Knights of the Round Table. A legend is in many ways very similar to a myth. It is a story handed from one generation to another by word of mouth. The difference is that a legend is often thought to be based on real people and real events.

This famous Celtic legend is probably based on Arthur, a famous warrior of the fifth century who led the Britons in their struggle against the Saxons.

According to the story, Arthur became king when he pulled a sword from a stone. Over the following years he gathered around him brave and noble knights who had many great adventures.

Many of the original stories about King Arthur are well known today from TV and films. One story tells of how Arthur came by his famous sword, Excalibur, whilst out riding with the magician, Merlin. Because this version was written over five hundred years ago, some of the words may seem strange and unfamiliar to you. Read the passage carefully.

Le Morte D'Arthur

And as they rode, King Arthur said, 'I have no sword.'

'No force,' said Merlin, 'hereby is a sword that shall be yours, and I may.'

So they rode till they came to a lake that was a fair water and broad.
5 And in the midst Arthur was ware of an arm clothed in white samite, that held a fair sword in that hand.

'Lo,' said Merlin, 'yonder is the sword that I spoke of.'

So with that they saw a damosel going upon the lake.

'What damosel is that?' said Arthur.

10 'That is the Lady of the Lake,' said Merlin. 'And within that lake there is a great rock, and therein is as fair a palace as any on earth, and richly beseen. And this damosel will come to you anon; and then speak ye fair to her that she may give you that sword.'

So anon came this damosel to Arthur and saluted him, and he her
15 again.

'Damosel,' said Arthur, 'what sword is that yonder that the arm holdeth above the water? I would it were mine, for I have no sword.'

'Sir Arthur,' said the damosel, 'that sword is mine. And if ye will give me a gift when I ask it you, ye shall have it.'

20 'By my faith,' said Arthur, 'I will give you what gift that ye will ask.'

'Well,' said the damosel. 'Go ye into yonder barge and row yourself to the sword, and take it and the scabbard with you; and I will ask my gift when I see my time.'

So King Arthur and Merlin alit and tied their horses unto two trees,
25 and so they went into the barge; and when they came to the sword that the hand held, then King Arthur took it up by the handles and bore it with him, and the arm and the hand went under the water. And so he came unto the land and rode forth.

Then King Arthur looked on the sword and liked it passing well. Then
30 said Merlin, 'Whether like ye better the sword or the scabbard?'

'I like better the sword,' said Arthur.

'Ye are the more unwise, for the scabbard is worth ten of the sword; for while ye have the scabbard upon you, ye shall lose no blood be ye never so sore wounded. Therefore keep well the scabbard always with you.'

from ***Le Morte D'Arthur*** *by Sir Thomas Malory*

Activity 4 WS ICT

Make a storyboard to show the key stages in the story. To make a storyboard you need to:

- divide your page into six
- choose the six main stages from the story
- draw a picture to show what is happening at each main stage
- write a sentence to explain what is happening.

Copy and complete the storyboard below. The first and last stages have been done for you.

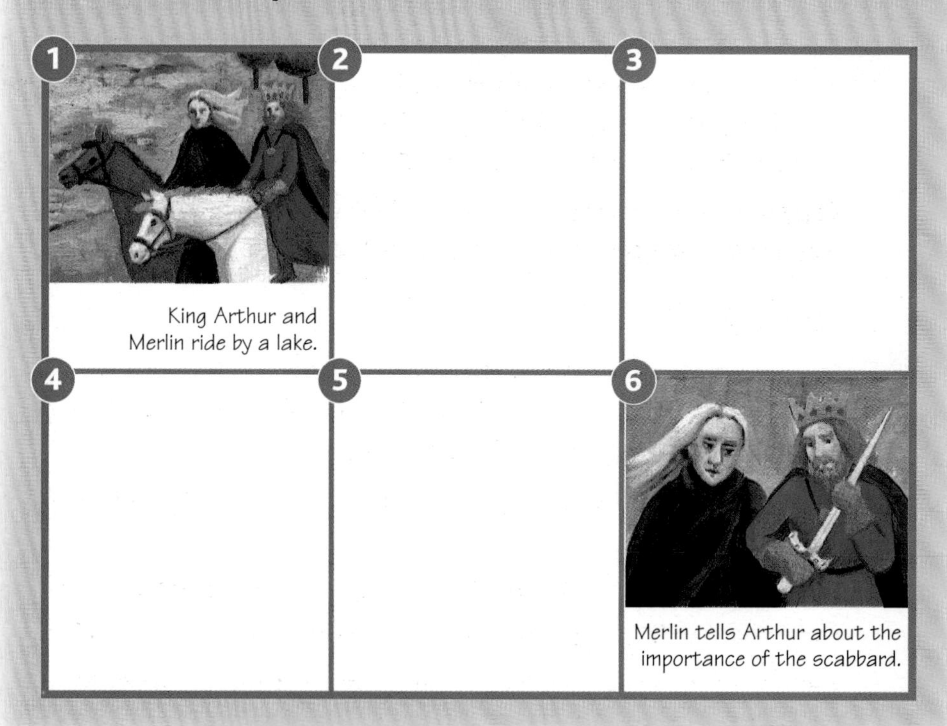

1
2
3
King Arthur and Merlin ride by a lake.
4
5
6
Merlin tells Arthur about the importance of the scabbard.

Activity 5 WS ICT

1 You may not recognise some of the words in the passage. This could be because:

- you have not learned them yet
- the words are **archaic** and rarely used now.

An example of a word you may not have learned yet is *samite* in line 5. This was a heavy silk material used for clothing in the Middle Ages.

An example of an archaic word is *ye*, first used in line 12. Today we would use *you* instead.

a Look at lines 1–15. List the words you do not know. Use a dictionary to help you find out their meanings.

b Now try writing lines 1–15 in modern English. You do not need to do a word-for-word update, but you do need to get the general feeling of what is being said. Here is an example of what you could do with the first two lines:

As they were riding along, King Arthur said, 'I haven't got a sword.'

'No problem,' said Merlin, 'There's a sword near here that you can have if I can fix it.'

2 It is not only the words in the passage that may be unfamiliar. You may have noticed something strange about:

- the order in which the words are used in the sentences. When Merlin asks Arthur whether he prefers the sword or the scabbard, Arthur replies; 'I like better the sword.' Nowadays we would say: 'I like the sword better.'
- the different way the words are used. The damosel (young woman) tells Arthur, 'Go ye into yonder barge and row yourself to the sword.' Nowadays we would probably say: 'Get in that boat and row to the sword.'

Copy out three sentences where you think words are used in an unusual way. Rewrite the sentences as you think they might be written today.

Activity 6 ICT

1 Now that you have looked at a range of stories from the past, and thought about some from the present, make a list of the ingredients you think are needed to make a good story.

2 Write your own story or design a cartoon sketch in which the following ingredients appear:

- a monster
- a hero or heroine
- a fight between good and evil.

Your story can be set in the past or in modern times.

Remember to gather your ideas together and put them in order before you start to write.

2 Ways into poetry

This unit will help you to:
- recognise and appreciate a range of poetic **forms**
- think about the links between form and content
- develop an understanding of how poets use **rhyme**, **repetition**, **similes** and sound.

It is possible to write a poem about any idea, thought or feeling. Read the following poems and extracts from poems a few times, first silently and then aloud. Write down your response to each poem.

It is Night

It is night
and the stars
Hang loosely in the sky.
As if
at any moment
the slender thread might break
and they would fall.
Making a heap of light in the dark street.

Janice E. Parkin

You Say

You say I am mysterious.
Let me explain myself:
In a land of oranges
I am faithful to apples.

Elsa Gidlow

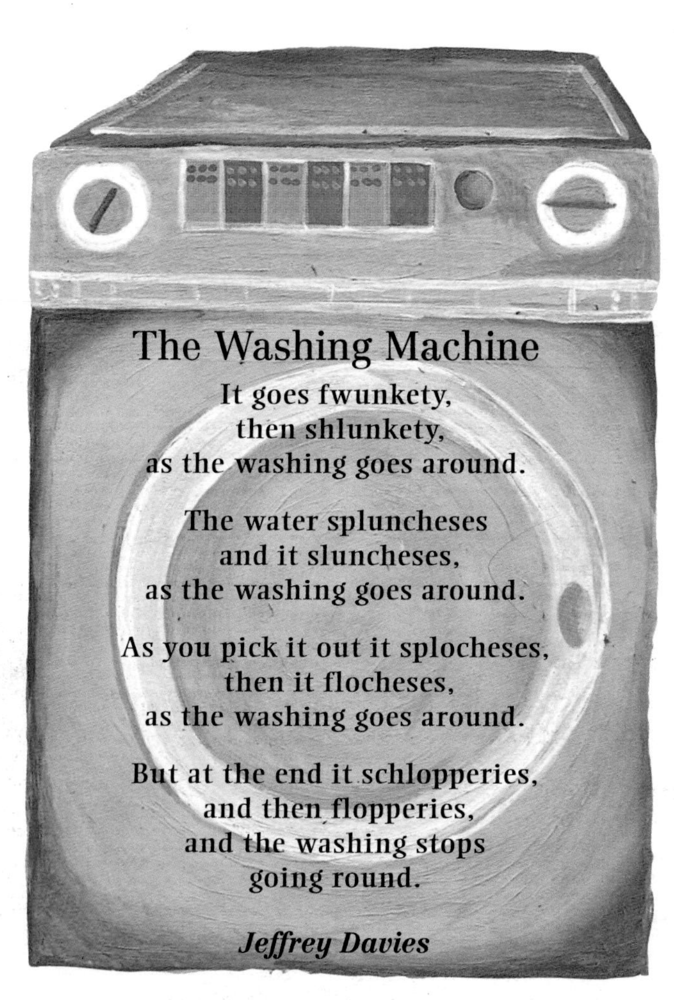

The Washing Machine

It goes fwunkety,
then shlunkety,
as the washing goes around.

The water spluncheses
and it sluncheses,
as the washing goes around.

As you pick it out it splocheses,
then it flocheses,
as the washing goes around.

But at the end it schlopperies,
and then flopperies,
and the washing stops
going round.

Jeffrey Davies

Word bank

tyrant – cruel and all powerful
drear – gloomy

Spellbound

The night is darkening round me,
The wild winds coldly blow;
But a **tyrant** spell has bound me
And I cannot, cannot go.

5 The giant trees are bending
Their bare boughs weighed with snow.
And the storm is fast descending,
And yet I cannot go.

Clouds beyond clouds above me,
10 Wastes beyond wastes below;
But nothing **drear** can move me;
I will not, cannot go.

Emily Brontë

One

Only one of me
and nobody can get a second one
from a photocopy machine.

Nobody has the fingerprints I have.
5 Nobody can cry my tears, or laugh my laugh
or have my expectancy when I wait.

But anybody can mimic my dance with my dog.
Anybody can howl how I sing out of tune.
And mirrors can show me multiplied
10 many times, say, dressed up in red
or dressed up in grey.

Nobody can get into my clothes for me
or feel my fall for me, or do my running.
Nobody hears my music for me, either.

15 I am just this one.
Nobody else makes the words
I shape with sound, when I talk.

But anybody can act how I stutter in a rage.
Anybody can copy echoes I make.
20 And mirrors can show me multiplied
many times, say, dressed up in green
or dressed up in blue.

James Berry

Activity 1 WS ICT

Discuss the poems in pairs or small groups. As a starting point you could talk about:

- the pictures they create for you
- words that sound interesting
- what the poems mean to you.

Once you have talked about each of the poems, decide how you could represent each poem as a picture. What would your picture look like for each poem?

Poetry can mean different things to different people. Sometimes you can understand a poem straight away and sometimes it takes a lot of thought and effort. Sometimes a poem can have an instant and strong effect on your feelings without you really knowing why. Sometimes your view of a poem will depend on:

- your age when you read it
- what is happening in your life at that time.

Why do you think these two things might make a difference?

There are things you can learn about poetry which will help you to understand more about a poem's meaning, the way it has been written and why it affects you in a particular way.

Form

Poems come in all different shapes and sizes. This gives poets a lot of freedom to decide how they will put their words on the page. The shape of a poem and the way the words are arranged on the page are called the form. Here are three main types of poetic form:

Concrete or 'shape' poems

In concrete poetry, the poet places the words in particular positions on the page to give the poem extra impact. In a way, the poet is experimenting with how the words look on the page.

Activity 2

Look at the two poems opposite.

What is unusual about the way the poets have set out their ideas?

How does the bundle of words in *Superstink* give you a better sense of the smell than if the words had been set out in lines?

Why do you think the poet chose to set out *Revolver* in a circle? Think about both the gun and the meaning of revolve.

These poems are meant to be looked at but they can be read aloud. Have a go!

SUPERSTINK

Big bus at the bus stop.

Ready to go again.

Big noise.

Big cloud of

aaargh

shudder gasp cough gulp

stifle

stench retch wheeze

sniffle snuffle strangle choke

@?&%

poison choke

katchooo

catarrh sneeze ghughughughu

Robert Froman

REVOLVER

Allan Riddell

Stanzas
Sometimes poems are organised into clearly separate blocks, in the same way that prose writing is divided into **paragraphs**. These blocks in poetry are called **stanzas**. They can be short or long, the same length or different lengths. Here is an example of a poem divided into two equal stanzas:

Obstacles

I can't take no more, I can't stand it
I tell you, I've really had enough
How many times has this been said
When the going begins to get tough

5 So you turn your back on that problem
And for a while you're feeling strong
But you are right back where you started
When the next one comes along

Lorraine Simeon

Activity 3

Answer these questions to help you understand why the poet has divided the poem into two separate stanzas:

a What is the first stanza about?
b Who is the first stanza about?
c What is the second stanza about?
d Who is the second stanza about?

Free verse
Sometimes the use of stanzas can restrict what a poet wants to say. Some poems are written in a less formal way using a form of poetry known as **free verse**. *At the Match. Harry's Monologue.* is an example of a poem written like this.

Read the poem carefully.

Harry is clearly very excited by the football match and the things that happen before it starts. How do you feel when you're excited? What happens to the way you speak? Do the words come tumbling out?

It is this sense of excitement that the poet wants to get across. He uses the word *and* a lot in order to create the sense of one idea following quickly on from another. The use of stanzas would create breaks in the way the poem is read. It would stop the flow of words and the sense of the words tumbling out in excitement. By using free verse, the poet is able to give the impression of actual speech and of the sensation of being there at the match.

At the Match. Harry's Monologue

HARRY: Come Saturday,
The whole town comes alive,
People are going one way,
From all the streets,
5 They are going the one way,
And meeting and joining,
And going on and meeting more and more
Till the trickle becomes a flood.
And men are packed so tight
10 That cars have to nose their way through.
And you come to the stadium,
And it's humming,
A hum comes from the bowl.
And the people inside seem to be saying,
15 Come on in, come on in,
And you jostle at the turnstile,
And the turnstile clicks and clicks,
And push nearer and nearer,
Through the dark gap,
20 Then you're in.
And the great stand of the City End,
It's like a hall,
A great hall,
And you go on,
25 Through the arch
And you see the pitch,
Green, new shaven and watered,
And the groundsman's made the white lines,
As straight as a ruler,
30 And the ash is pressed.
And you find your place among the fans,
The real fans,
The singers and chanters and rattle wavers.
And a sheet of tobacco smoke hangs over the crowd.
35 And the crowd whistles and hoots,
And the policemen circling the pitch
Look up and know they're in for a rough day of it,
And the stadium fills up,
The Open End first, then the City End,
40 Then the paddock, then the covered seated stand,
Then, last of all, the fat directors
With the Lord Mayor and cigars.
And the reporters are in their little glass box,
And the cameramen position themselves
45 By the goal,
And there's a looking down the tunnel,
Then a hush.
Then out they come.
The lads,
50 Like toy footballers on a green billiard table.
And the roar goes up ...

Peter Terson

Activity 4 ICT

Prepare a group reading of *At the Match. Harry's Monologue*.

In groups of three or four, study the poem carefully and decide where to put the natural breaks in the speech. You might, for instance, want to pause at the end of line 2 and then at the end of line 8. Now think about how each section could be read aloud. What tone of voice would you use? Which bits could you say loudly and which bits quietly, which bits quickly and which bits slowly? Are there any lines which you could read together? Once you have thought about these choices, decide which lines each of you is going to read. Then practise your reading.

Devices

As well as learning about the ways poems may be set out on the page, it is useful to be aware of some of the features that are common to many poems. These are often called poetic **devices**.

Rhyme and repetition

Roger McGough wrote the following poem after reading the newspaper headline

U.S. Flies in Hamburgers

which was about hamburgers being airlifted to U.S Marines. Read it carefully.

U.S. Flies in Hamburgers

If you go down the High Street today
You'll be sure of a big surprise.
When you order your favourite burger
With a milkshake and regular fries.

5 For the secret is out
I tell you no lies
They've stopped using beef
In favour of FLIES

FLIES, FLIES, big juicy FLIES,
10 FLIES as American as apple pies.

Horseflies, from Texas, as big as your thumb
Are sautéed with onions and served in a bun.

Free-range bluebottles, carefully rinsed
Are smothered in garlic, and painlessly minced.

15 Black-eyed bees with stings intact
Add a zesty zing, and that's a fact.

Colorado beetles, ants from Kentucky,
Rhode Island roaches, and if you're unlucky

Baltimore bedbugs (and even horrider)
20 Leeches as squashy as peaches from Florida.

FLIES, FLIES, big juicy FLIES,
FLIES as American as mom's apple pies.

It's lovely down in MacDingles today
But if you don't fancy flies
25 Better I'd say to keep well away
Stay home and eat Birds' Eyes.

Roger McGough

Word bank
sautéed – shallow-fried
roaches – cockroaches

Activity 5 WS ICT

Rhyme

1 Words rhyme when they end with the same sound. In poetry, the words that rhyme are often placed at the ends of the lines. In the first stanza, the words that rhyme are:

surprise fries.

Write down the pairs of words that rhyme in the rest of the poem.

2 Sometimes rhyming words are also found within the same line. This is called **internal rhyme**. In line 10, the words that rhyme are:

flies pies.

Which words rhyme in lines 20 and 25?

3 Rhyme sometimes connects things you might not normally connect. Sometimes rhymes can make you laugh. Make your own list of rhyming words that suggest something horrible together with something nice, for example:

mould gold.

Repetition

4 Poets often repeat words, phrases (groups of words) and whole lines in poems. They may do this:

- to emphasise a point
- to create the type of chorus you might find in a song.

Look back at *U.S. Flies in Hamburgers*. Which lines are repeated? Why do you think the poet did this?

5 Try reading the poem aloud in small groups or as a class. Decide who will read which lines, but make sure that you all read lines 9–10 and lines 21–22. Notice how some words are in capital letters to make them stand out. How do you think you should read these particular words?

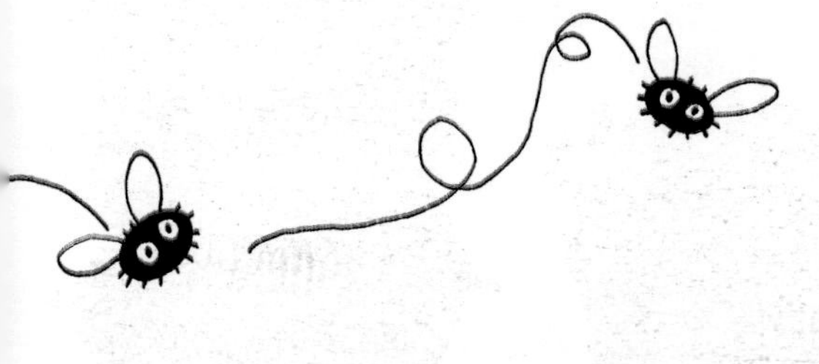

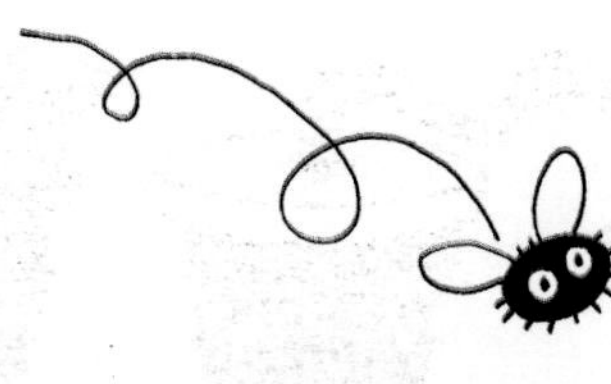

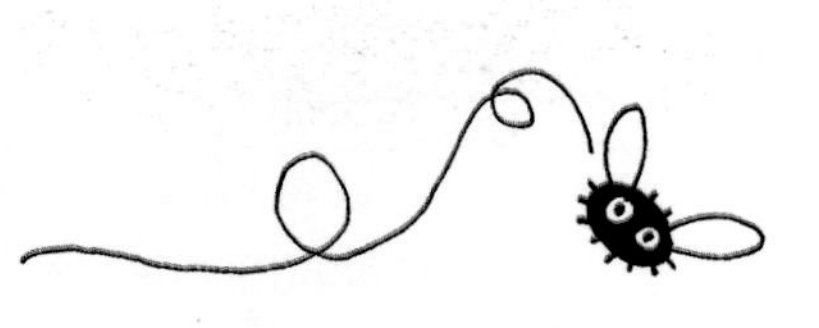

Similes

Sometimes a poet will create an **image** in order to make an idea clearer, for example by saying that something is like something else. This is known as a simile. Read the following poem carefully:

The Fly

How large unto the tiny fly
Must little things appear!
A rosebud like a feather bed,
Its prickle like a spear;

5 A dewdrop like a looking-glass,
A hair like golden wire;
The smallest grain of mustard-seed
As fierce as coals of fire;

A loaf of bread, a lofty hill;
10 A wasp, a cruel leopard;
And specks of salt as bright to see
As lambkins to a shepherd.

Walter de la Mare

Activity 6 WS ICT

1 Copy and complete the following table:

The thing	What it is compared with
a rosebud	a feather bed
a rosebud's prickle	a spear
a dewdrop	
a hair	
a grain of mustard seed	
a loaf of bread	
a wasp	
specks of salt	

2 The poet is trying to describe what things must look like to a fly. What does he show you by the comparisons he makes?

Think about how a giant might see things, in comparison with the way we see them. Write similes that a giant might use to describe the following:

an ocean is like ...
a cathedral as tall as ...
a mountain is like ...
a person as small as ...
a shopping centre as busy as ...
a forest is like ...

Word sounds

Poets use words in unusual ways and experiment with sounds. This is one of the reasons why it is so important to read poetry aloud. Read the following poem aloud:

Muddy Boots

Trudging down the country lane,
Splodgely thlodgely plooph.
Two foot deep in slimy mud,
Fallomph Polopf Gallooph.
Hopolosplodgely go your boots,
5 Slopthopy gruthalamie golumph.
Then you find firm ground again,
Plonky shlonky clonky.
BUT ... then you sink back in again,
Squelchy crathpally hodgle.
10

Sitting outside scraping your boots,
Sclapey gulapy criketty,
Cursing the horrible six-inch slodge,
Scrapey flakey cakey.
15 Flakes of mud, crispling off the boots,
Crinkey splinky schlinkle.
Never again, will I venture into that
... Schlodgely, Flopchely, Thlodgely,
schrinkshely, slimy, grimy, squelchy,
20 ghastly MUD!

Philip Paddon

Activity 7 ICT

In this poem, the poet is trying to capture the sound and the feeling of walking in thick mud.

1 Make a list of the words he uses to describe these sensations. Which of these words are made up?

2 Think about the words that describe the sound and feeling of being two foot deep in mud:
Fallomph Polopf Gallooph
and the words that describe being on firm ground again:
Plonky shlonky clonky.
What is the difference between the two sets of words?
How do their sounds emphasise the sounds that are being described?

3 Try making up your own words to describe the sound and feeling of running through water. (You will find some other unusual uses of sound in *The Washing Machine* on page 22.)

Activity 8 ICT

Look back at all the poems in this unit. Which ones did you like best? What features do you think make a good poem? Try writing a poem of your own, using some or all of these features. Ask your friends to read your poem and tell you what they think of it.

3 Thinking about people and places

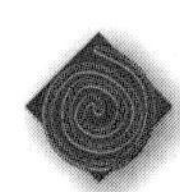

This unit will help you to:
- learn about the different techniques used by writers
- understand how words can describe atmosphere
- refer to the text when explaining viewpoint
- understand how choice of words affects meaning.

Describing people

Writers give a lot of time and thought to the way they describe people. They have to try to make them seem real to the reader and, to do this, they must choose their words very carefully. In this section you will look at some of the different ways writers describe people.

Sometimes writers describe the appearance of a character in great detail. You have already met the character of Merlin when reading about King Arthur on pages 19–20. Read the following detailed description of the wizard Merlin. This is a twentieth-century version, and the author has spelled his name Merlyn.

The Sword in the Stone

The old gentleman was a singular spectacle. He was dressed in a flowing gown with fur tippets which had the signs of the zodiac embroidered all over it, together with various cabalistic signs, as of triangles with eyes in them, queer crosses, leaves of trees, bones and
5 birds and animals and a planetarium whose stars shone like bits of looking glass with the sun on them. He had a pointed hat like a dunce's cap, or like the headgear worn by ladies of that time, except that the ladies were accustomed to have a bit of veil floating from the top of it. He also had a wand of lignum vitae, which he had laid down in the
10 grass beside him, and a pair of horn-rimmed spectacles. They were extraordinary spectacles, being without ear pieces, but shaped rather like scissors or the antennae of the tarantula wasp.

Merlyn had a long white beard and long white moustache which hung down on either side of it,
15 and close inspection showed that he was far from clean. It was not that he had dirty finger-nails or anything like that, but some large bird seemed to have been nesting in his hair. The old man was streaked with droppings over his shoulders,
20 among the stars and triangles of his gown, and a large spider was slowly lowering itself from the tip of his hat, as he gazed and slowly blinked at the little boy in front of him.

from ***The Sword in the Stone*** *by T.H.White*

Word bank

a singular spectacle – an unusual sight

tippets – a trim on the sleeves and hood

cabalistic signs – secret signs associated with science and religion

planetarium – a model of the solar system

lignum vitae – the wood of life (Latin)

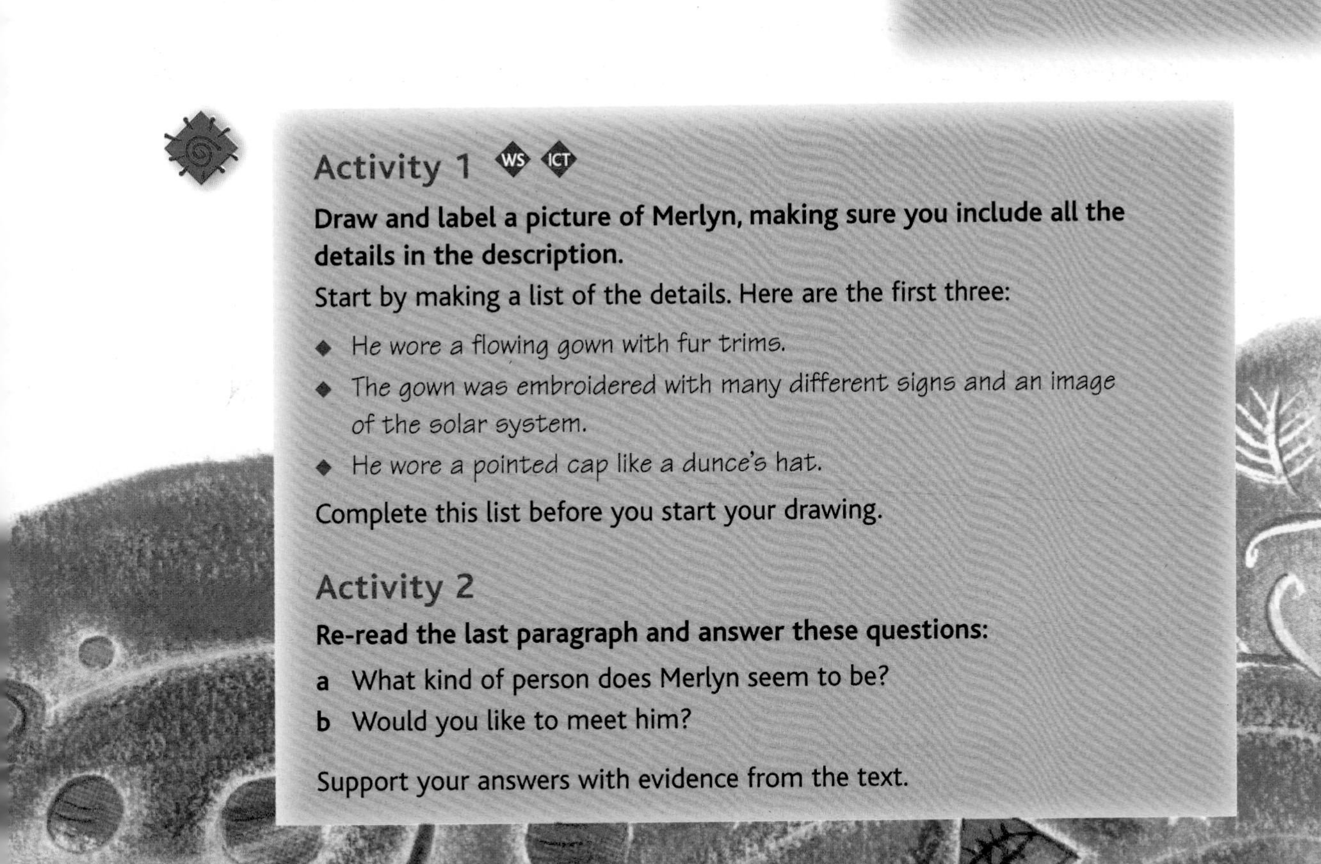

Activity 1 WS ICT

Draw and label a picture of Merlyn, making sure you include all the details in the description.

Start by making a list of the details. Here are the first three:

- *He wore a flowing gown with fur trims.*
- *The gown was embroidered with many different signs and an image of the solar system.*
- *He wore a pointed cap like a dunce's hat.*

Complete this list before you start your drawing.

Activity 2

Re-read the last paragraph and answer these questions:

a What kind of person does Merlyn seem to be?

b Would you like to meet him?

Support your answers with evidence from the text.

A character's appearance will often tell you something about the kind of person they are. In the following extract, thirteen-year-old Buddy is about to go to school with his dad to meet his teacher, Mr Normington.

Buddy

Buddy thought he was going to die, when his dad came downstairs ready to go at six-thirty. He was dressed in his complete Teddy Boy outfit – drainpipe trousers, drape jacket with velvet collar, bootlace tie, thick crepe-soled shoes and fluorescent green socks. His hair was
5 slicked back with oil and it was obvious that he'd taken great care to look as tidy as possible. He'd dressed himself in his 'best' for the occasion.

'I thought you had to go straight out afterwards,' Buddy said, not daring to come to the point but hoping his dad
10 might change his mind and put on something else. Jeans – anything would be better than this.

'I am. Got me other stuff in 'ere,' he said, holding up a Woolworth's plastic bag.

Buddy's stomach turned to water and he felt sick. The
15 evening was going to be a disaster. 'Dad,' he said weakly.

'What?'

'Can't you put something else on?'

'Why?'

20 'Well, it's just ... Mr Normington ... won't like it.'

'He'll 'ave to lump it then, won't he?' There was defiance in his dad's voice but a touch of sadness, too, and Buddy knew he'd hurt him.

The walk to school seemed to take ages.
25 His dad was right. What did it matter what Mr Normington thought? It wasn't as if his dad looked scruffy or dirty – he looked really smart. But he did look different. Even some of the people in the street looked twice as they walked past.

*from **Buddy** by Nigel Hinton*

Word bank

Teddy Boy – a popular fashion for young people in the mid-1950s

Activity 3 WS

Answer the following questions:

1 What do the clothes show about Buddy's dad?

2 How do you know Buddy's dad has made a special effort?

3 How do you think Buddy's dad felt when Buddy asked him to change his clothes?

4 What does Buddy think about his dad's appearance? Think carefully before answering.

5 What do you learn about both Buddy and his dad from this extract?

Writers do not always give such a detailed description of the appearance of a character. In the following description of Scrooge, Charles Dickens uses a different method to reveal his character to the reader. You maybe couldn't draw a picture of him, but you get a very good impression of the kind of person he is. Read the description and then complete the activity on the next page.

A Christmas Carol

Oh! but he was a tight-fisted hand at the grindstone. Scrooge! A squeezing, wrenching, grasping, scraping, clutching, covetous, old sinner! Hard and sharp as flint, from which no steel had ever struck out generous fire; secret, and self-contained, and solitary as an oyster. The cold within
5 him froze his old features, nipped his pointed nose, shrivelled his cheek, stiffened his gait; made his eyes red, his thin lips blue; and spoke out shrewdly in his grating voice. A frosty rime was on his head, and on his eyebrows, and his wiry chin. He carried his own low temperature always about with him; he iced his office in the dog-days, and didn't thaw it one
10 degree at Christmas.

External heat and cold had little influence on Scrooge. No warmth could warm, no wintry weather chill him. No wind that blew was bitterer than he, no falling snow
15 was more intent upon its purpose, no pelting rain less open to entreaty. Foul weather didn't know where to have him. The heaviest rain, and snow, and hail, and sleet, could boast of the advantage over him in only
20 one respect. They often 'came down' handsomely and Scrooge never did.

*from **A Christmas Carol** by Charles Dickens*

Word bank

covetous – envious of other people's possessions

frosty rime – white hair looking like frost

dog-days – the hottest period in summer

'came down' handsomely – **a)** fell heavily **b)** gave money generously

Activity 4 WS ICT

In this activity you will look at the techniques Dickens uses to create the character of Scrooge.

1 **Use of adjectives**

Writers often use adjectives to tell you more about a person. Look at the way Scrooge is described in the opening sentences of the paragraph:

Oh! but he was a tight-fisted hand at the grindstone. Scrooge! A squeezing, wrenching, grasping, scraping, clutching, covetous, old sinner!

The words that are underlined are adjectives. They tell you more about the kind of person Scrooge was.

What do these adjectives tell you about Scrooge? Use a dictionary to find out the meaning of words you do not know.

What is the effect of Dickens' use of so many adjectives together?

2 **Use of imagery**

a similes

Dickens uses two similes in his description of Scrooge:

Hard and sharp as flint, from which no steel had ever struck out generous fire; secret, and self-contained, and solitary as an oyster.

What do these two similes tell you about Scrooge?

b images of coldness

Dickens uses images of coldness to show the reader what kind of person Scrooge was.

What images of coldness can you find in lines 11–21?
What do these images add to your impression of Scrooge?

3 **Use of repetition**

In the following lines Dickens uses repetition to emphasise a point he wishes to make about Scrooge's character:

No warmth could warm, no wintry weather chill him. No wind that blew was bitterer than he, no falling snow was more intent upon its purpose, no pelting rain less open to entreaty.

What word does Dickens repeat in these sentences?
What idea is he trying to get across to the reader?

Sometimes a writer will use **contrast** to emphasise something about the appearance of a character. In the following extract, a young boy, Luke, is hiding in a hall filled with witches:

The Witches

All the women, or rather the witches, were now sitting motionless in their chairs and staring as though hypnotised at somebody who had suddenly appeared on the platform. That somebody was another woman.

The first thing I noticed about this woman was her size. She was tiny,
5 probably no more than four and a half feet tall. She looked quite young, I guessed about twenty-five or six, and she was very pretty. She had on a rather stylish long black dress that reached right to the ground and she wore black gloves that came up to her elbows. Unlike the others, she wasn't wearing a hat.

10 She didn't look to me like a witch at all, but she couldn't possibly *not* be one, otherwise what on earth was she doing up there on the platform? And why, for heaven's sake, were all the other witches gazing at her with such a mixture of adoration, awe and fear?

Very slowly, the young lady on the platform raised her hands to her face. I
15 saw her gloved fingers unhooking something behind her ears, and then ... then she caught hold of her cheeks and lifted her face clean away! The whole of that pretty face came away in her hands!

It was a mask!

What do you learn about the appearance of the young woman in lines 4–9?
What clues are given to make you think that there is something suspicious about her?
Now turn to the next page and read on:

As she took off the mask, she turned sideways and placed it carefully upon
20 a small table near by, and when she turned round again and faced us, I very nearly screamed out loud.

That face of hers was the most frightful and frightening thing I have ever seen. Just looking at it gave me the shakes all over. It was so crumpled and wizened, so shrunken and shrivelled, it looked as though it had been
25 pickled in vinegar. It was a fearsome and ghastly sight. There was something terribly wrong with it, something foul and putrid and decayed. It seemed quite literally to be rotting away at the edges, and in the middle of the face, around the mouth and cheeks, I could see the skin all cankered and worm-eaten, as though maggots were working away in there.

30 There are times when something is so frightful you become mesmerised by it and can't look away. I was like that now. I was transfixed. I was numbed. I was magnetised by the sheer horror of this woman's features. But there was more to it than that. There was a look of serpents in those eyes of hers as they flashed around the audience.

35 I knew immediately, of course, that this was none other than The Grand High Witch herself. I knew also why she had worn a mask. She could never have moved around in public, let alone book in at an hotel, with her real face. Everyone who saw her would have run away screaming.

from ***The Witches*** *by Roald Dahl*

Activity 5 WS

In this activity you will look at the techniques the author uses to describe The Grand High Witch.

1 **Use of adjectives**

Copy out lines 22–26 from the passage and underline the adjectives used to describe the witch's face. What do the adjectives tell you about The Grand High Witch?

Now rewrite your extract, using different adjectives to describe a beautiful and good witch. Is there anything else you need to change?

2 **Use of repetition**

How does the author use repetition to emphasise the little boy's horror at the sight of the witch's face? Copy out the sentences that show you this.

3 **Use of contrast**

Why do you think the author presents the reader with two very different descriptions of the same person?

Describing places

As well as taking great care to describe their characters, writers give a lot of time and thought to how they describe the **setting**. The setting is the surroundings in which the action takes place. In this section you will look at some of the different ways writers use setting.

For a play to be produced on stage, the writer needs to give details of the setting. These details are included in the stage directions. Read the following:

Scene 5

The old barn. Wooden. Cobwebs at a broken window. A scatter of tools.
A wheelbarrow. An old feeding trough. A big pile of hay. A cartwheel etc.
A great place to play.

from ***Blue Remembered Hills*** *by Dennis Potter*

Activity 6 ICT

Imagine that you have been asked to produce this play. Draw and label a sketch of the setting you would want for this scene.

Before starting your sketch, think carefully about the following:

- What details in the stage directions suggest that the barn is neglected?
- What is suggested by *a scatter of tools*?

You need to include the details given to you by the playwright, but notice that he has also given you a lot of freedom when he writes *A cartwheel etc. A great place to play*. This allows you to add in many details of your own choosing.

Once you have decided on the appearance of the setting, think about what the place feels like. Look back at the stage directions. Which of the following words captures the feel of the place?

◆ lonely ◆ playful ◆ sad ◆ neglected ◆ exciting
◆ forlorn ◆ dangerous ◆ happy

Try to make your sketch match the feel.

In a play the setting is described to give an idea of what the place looks and feels like. Setting is equally important in **prose**. Read the following extract which tells you about Harry Potter's new school, Hogwarts. When Harry goes there, he finds that things are not quite as he expected them to be:

Harry Potter and the Philosopher's Stone

There were a hundred and
forty-two staircases at Hogwarts:
wide, sweeping ones; narrow, rickety ones;
some that led somewhere different
5 on a Friday; some with a vanishing step
half-way up that you had to remember to jump.
Then there were doors that wouldn't open unless
you asked politely, or tickled them in exactly the
right place, and doors that weren't really doors at all,
10 but solid walls just pretending. It was also very hard to
remember where anything was, because it all seemed to move
around a lot. The people in the portraits kept going to visit
each other and Harry was sure the coats of armour could walk.

*from **Harry Potter and the Philosopher's Stone** by J.K.Rowling*

Activity 7

1 Check that you have understood the extract by answering these questions:

a How many staircases are there at Hogwarts?

b What different types of staircase are there?

c What is unusual about the doors?

d Why is it hard to remember where anything is?

2 What kind of place do you imagine Hogwarts to be? What is it about the description that makes you think this?

Use of adjectives

Writers often use adjectives to tell you more about a particular place or thing. Look at the way the staircases are described in the opening sentence of the extract on the previous page. The words that are underlined are adjectives. They give you more information about the types of staircase.

There were a hundred and forty-two staircases at Hogwarts: wide, sweeping ones; narrow, rickety ones; some that led somewhere different on a Friday; some with a vanishing step half-way up that you had to remember to jump.

How do these adjectives help you to get a clearer image of the place in your mind?

Read the following extract in which Harry visits the dining hall:

Harry had never even imagined such a strange and splendid place.
It was lit by thousands and thousands of candles which were floating
in mid-air over four long tables, where the rest of the students
were sitting. These tables were laid with glittering golden plates
5 and goblets. At the top of the hall was another long table
where the teachers were sitting. Professor McGonagall
led the first years up here, so that they came to a halt in
a line facing the other students, with the teachers behind
them. The hundreds of faces staring at them looked
10 like pale lanterns in the flickering candlelight.
Dotted here and there among the students, the
ghosts shone misty silver. Mainly to avoid all the
staring eyes, Harry looked upwards and saw
a velvety black ceiling dotted with stars.

from ***Harry Potter and the Philosopher's Stone***
by J.K.Rowling

Activity 8 WS

1 Read the passage again. Make a list of all the adjectives in the passage.

2 The adjectives tell you a lot about the kind of place the dining hall is. They help to create a particular kind of feeling or atmosphere. Look at the words you have listed. What kind of atmosphere do they create? Choose two of the following words:

◆ wonderful ◆ ordinary ◆ evil ◆ horrible ◆ amazing
◆ mysterious ◆ miserable ◆ magical

3 Now rewrite the passage, replacing some of the adjectives used by the writer with adjectives of your own. Try to give the place a frightening and dangerous atmosphere.

In the descriptions of setting that you have read so far, the writers have focused on the physical surroundings. Sometimes, though, it is the weather that is the most important feature of the setting. The novel *Rice without Rain* starts with a description of a place where there has been no rain for a long time:

Rice without Rain

Heat the colour of fire, sky as heavy as mud, and under both the soil – hard, dry, unyielding.

It was a silent harvest. Across the valley, yellow rice fields stretched, stooped and dry. The sun glazed the afternoon with a heat so fierce that the
5 distant mountains shimmered in it. The dust in the sky, the cracked earth, the shrivelled leaves fluttering on brittle branches – everything was scorched. ...

A single lark flew by, casting a swift shadow on the stubbled fields. From under the brim of her hat, Jinda saw it wing its way west.

A good sign, Jinda thought. Maybe the harvest won't be so poor after
10 all. She straightened up, feeling prickles of pain shoot up her spine, and gazed at the brown fields before her. In all her seventeen years, Jinda had never seen a crop as bad as this one. The heads of grain were so light the rice stalks were hardly bent under their weight. Jinda peeled the husk of one grain open: the rice grain inside was no thicker than a fingernail.

Activity 9 ICT

You are going to look at the detail in the description. First reread the opening sentence:

Heat the colour of fire, sky as heavy as mud,
and under both the soil – hard, dry, unyielding.

Here the writer gets across just how very hot it was by saying it was *the colour of fire*. Imagine a fire and you start to see and feel the heat she is describing.

1 Now think about mud and what it feels like. The sky is described as being *as heavy as mud*. What do you imagine the sky to be like?

2 The writer chooses three adjectives to describe the soil: *hard, dry, unyielding*. What does the word *unyielding* tell you about the soil?

3 The writer starts the second paragraph by saying *It was a silent harvest*. What do you think she means by this?

4 Find the word 'glazed' in line 4. What does it mean? How does it add to the feeling of heat?

5 Which words in lines 5–6 are used to give a feeling of dryness?

6 Read lines 12–14 . How is the rice affected by the dryness?

When the much-needed rain finally comes, things are very different. Read the next extract:

Jinda slithered down the steps of the verandah and ran towards the swinging bamboo gate. The earth was soft and pliant under her bare feet. How good to feel mud again, Jinda thought.

Out in the lane the wind was stronger, and a gust slashed against her arms like long sharp rice stalks. She passed the hibiscus hedge, and saw its leaves streaked a bright green where the rain had washed off the thick layers of dust. A few flowers burst through, cleansed a brilliant scarlet by the rain.

Sprinting down the lane, Jinda's steps were light and springy against the mud-slick soil. She felt the wind against her face, whipping her hair behind her, piercing through her thin wet clothes so that they felt like a second skin on her.

...

And still the rain quickened, pelting at the flat earth from the cloud-flattened sky.

Through the storm Jinda ran on. Running, she gulped in great mouthfuls of the wind, and felt the rain soak her clothes to her skin. Running, she felt the hard dry knot within her uncoil and grow soft and pliant again. She ran until her sides hurt, and her breath came in painful gasps.

The village lay far behind. Before her the rice fields stretched out, reaching to the foot of the mountains. Bathed in wet shadow, the mountains glowed a vibrant lilac.

*from **Rice without Rain** by Minfong Ho*

Activity 10 WS ICT

The second extract presents a very different picture of the setting. Copy and complete the following table, filling in the missing words from both extracts. The first one is done for you.

Extract 1	Extract 2
the soil – hard, dry, unyielding	the earth was soft and pliant
Across the valley, yellow rice fields stretched, ... and ...	Before her the rice fields stretched out, ... to the ....
the distant mountains	the mountains glowed a ....
the shrivelled leaves fluttering on	A few flowers burst through, ...
She straightened up, feeling	Sprinting down the lane, Jinda's steps were ....

4 Assignment 1

Spend about 1 hour on this.
Read the first part of the extract carefully and answer all the questions that follow it:

The Shilling Pie

Jim Jarvis hopped about on the edge of the road, his feet blue with cold. Passing carriages flung muddy snow up into his face and his eyes, and the swaying horses slithered and skidded as they were whipped on by their drivers. At last Jim saw his chance and made a dash for it through the traffic. The little shops in the dark street all glowed yellow with their hanging lamps, and Jim dodged from one light to the next until he came to the shop he was looking for. It was the meat pudding shop. Hungry boys and skinny dogs hovered round the doorway, watching for scraps. Jim pushed past them, his coin as hot as a piece of coal in his fist. He could hear his stomach gurgling as the rich smell of hot gravy met him.

Mrs Hodder was trying to sweep the soggy floor and sprinkle new straw down when Jim ran in.

'You can run right out again,' she shouted to him. 'If I'm not sick of little boys today!'

'But I've come to buy a pudding!' Jim told her. He danced up and down, opening his fist so his coin winked at her like an eye.

She prised it out of his hand and bit it. 'Where did you find this, little shrimp?' she asked him. 'And stop your dancing! You're making me rock like a ship at sea!'

Jim hopped onto a dry patch of straw. 'Ma's purse. And she said there won't be no more, because that's the last shilling we got, and I know that's true because I emptied it for her. So make it a good one, Mrs Hodder. Make it big, and lots of gravy!'

He ran home with the pie clutched to his chest, warming him through its cloth wrapping. Some of the boys outside the shop tried to chase him, but he soon lost them in the dark alleys, his heart thudding in case they caught him and stole the pie.

1 What details in the first two sentences tell you that the story is set in winter?

2 What other details are you given about the setting in the first paragraph?

3 What have you learned about:

- Mrs Hodder
- Jim's mother?

4 There are three similes in the passage. They are underlined. Copy them out and, for each one, explain the idea the writer is trying to get across to the reader.

Now read the second part of the extract and answer all the questions that follow it:

At last he came to his home, in a house so full of families that he
30 sometimes wondered how the floors and walls didn't come tumbling down with the weight and noise of them all. He ran up the stairs and burst into the room his own family lived in. He was panting with triumph and excitement.

'I've got the pie! I've got the pie!' he sang out.

35 'Sssh!' His sister Emily was kneeling on the floor, and she turned round to him sharply. 'Ma's asleep, Jim.'

Lizzie jumped up and ran to him, pulling him over towards the fire so they could spread out the pudding cloth on the hearth. They broke off chunks of pastry and dipped them into the brimming gravy.

40 'What about Ma?' asked Lizzie.

'She won't want it,' Emily said. 'She never eats.'

Lizzie pulled Jim's hand back as he was reaching out for another chunk. 'But the gravy might do her good,' she suggested. 'Just a little taste. Stop shovelling it down so fast, Jim. Let Ma have a bit.'

45 She turned round to her mother's pile of bedding and pulled back the ragged cover.

'Ma,' she whispered. 'Try a bit. It's lovely!'

She held a piece of gravy-soaked piecrust to her lips, but her mother shook her head and turned over, huddling her rug round her.

50 'I'll have it!' said Jim, but Lizzie put it on the corner of her mother's bed-rags.

'She might feel like it later,' she said. 'The smell might tempt her.'

'I told you,' said Emily. 'She don't want food no more. That's what she said.'

55 Jim paused for a moment in his eating, his hand resting over his portion of pie in case his sisters snatched it away from him. 'What's the matter with Ma?' he asked.

'Nothing's the matter,' said Emily. She chucked a log on the fire, watching how the flames curled themselves round it.

60 'She's tired, is all,' Lizzie prompted her. 'She just wants to sleep, don't she?'

'But she's been asleep all day,' Jim said. 'And yesterday. And the day before.'

'Just eat your pie,' said Emily. 'You heard what she said. There's no 65 more shillings in that purse, so don't expect no more pies after this one.'

'She'll get better soon,' Lizzie said. 'And then she'll be able to go back to work. There's lots of jobs for cooks. We'll soon be out of this place. That's what she told me, Jim.'

'Will we go back to our cottage?' Jim asked.

70 Lizzie shook her head. 'You know we can't go there, Jim. We had to move out when Father died.'

'Eat your pie,' said Emily. 'She wants us to enjoy it.'

But the pie had grown cold before the children finished it. They pulled their rag-pile close to the hearth and curled up together, Jim between 75 Emily and Lizzie. In all the rooms of the house they could hear people muttering and yawning and scratching. Outside in the street dogs were howling, and carriage wheels trundled on the slushy roads.

Jim lay awake. He could hear how his mother's breath rattled in her throat, and he knew by the way she tossed and turned that she wasn't 80 asleep. He could tell by the way his sisters lay taut and still each side of him that they were awake too, listening through the night to its noises, longing for day to come.

*from **Street Child** by Berlie Doherty*

5 What have you learned about:
- the place where the family live
- Jim's sisters?

6 *'She'll get better soon,' Lizzie said.* (line 66)

Do you think Lizzie is right? Give clear reasons for your answer.

Now think about both parts of the passage and answer these questions:

7 What clues can you find that tell you this story is set a long time ago?

8 Imagine you are Jim. Tell the story of the night you bought the shilling pie. You should include details of:
- what happened
- your thoughts and feelings.

A2 Reading non-fiction

Non-fiction texts are texts which are not poems, stories, novels or plays. They are not made up. There is a huge range of non-fiction texts. These include letters, diaries, leaflets, articles and adverts. People of all ages read non-fiction to learn about things and for enjoyment.

There are three units of work in this section:

The first unit, *Presentation of information*, introduces you to the range of non-fiction texts and looks at commonly-used presentational features. It will help you to identify these features and to appreciate the effects they have on the reader.

The second unit, *Finding out about non-fiction*, will help you to understand the terms *purpose* and *audience*. It will show you how to identify the purpose and audience of a non-fiction text and will increase your understanding of the differences between fact and opinion.

The third unit, *Reading for different purposes*, explores the different ways in which we read. It will help you to identify key points in a non-fiction text and to increase your awareness of different levels of meaning.

At the end of the section there is an assignment which tests you on the skills you will develop by working carefully through the three units.

5 Presentation of information

This unit will help you to:

- understand what is meant by non-fiction
- recognise the use of presentational features
- develop an awareness of how these features affect the reader.

Swimming-pool timetable

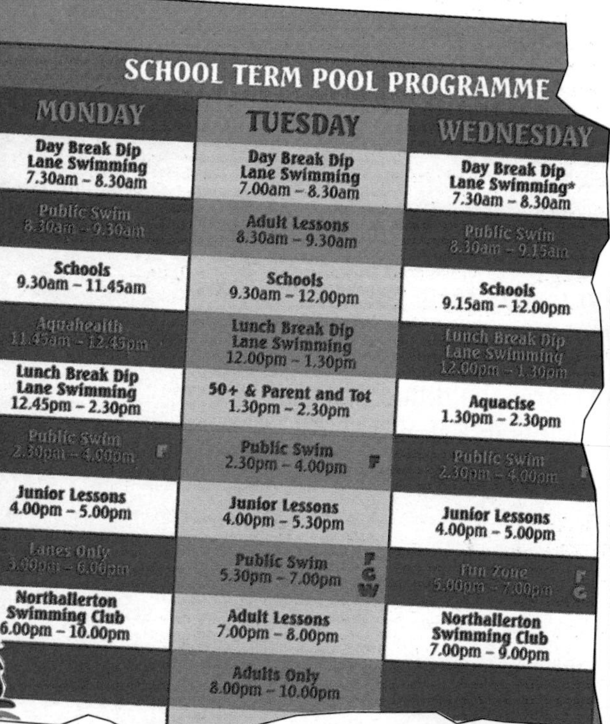

SCHOOL TERM POOL PROGRAMME

MONDAY	TUESDAY	WEDNESDAY
Day Break Dip Lane Swimming 7.30am – 8.30am	Day Break Dip Lane Swimming 7.00am – 8.30am	Day Break Dip Lane Swimming* 7.30am – 8.30am
Public Swim 8.30am – 9.30am	Adult Lessons 8.30am – 9.30am	Public Swim 8.30am – 9.15am
Schools 9.30am – 11.45am	Schools 9.30am – 12.00pm	Schools 9.15am – 12.00pm
Aquahealth 11.45am – 12.45pm	Lunch Break Dip Lane Swimming 12.00pm – 1.30pm	Lunch Break Dip Lane Swimming 12.00pm – 1.30pm
Lunch Break Dip Lane Swimming 12.45pm – 2.30pm	50+ & Parent and Tot 1.30pm – 2.30pm	Aquacise 1.30pm – 2.30pm
Public Swim 2.30pm – 4.00pm F	Public Swim 2.30pm – 4.00pm F	Public Swim 2.30pm – 4.00pm
Junior Lessons 4.00pm – 5.00pm	Junior Lessons 4.00pm – 5.30pm	Junior Lessons 4.00pm – 5.00pm
Lanes Only 5.00pm – 6.00pm	Public Swim 5.30pm – 7.00pm F G W	Fun Zone 5.00pm – 7.00pm F G
Northallerton Swimming Club 6.00pm – 10.00pm	Adult Lessons 7.00pm – 8.00pm	Northallerton Swimming Club 7.00pm – 9.00pm
	Adults Only 8.00pm – 10.00pm	

What are non-fiction texts?

Non-fiction texts are texts which are not poems, stories, novels or plays. They are not made up. People of all ages read non-fiction to learn about things and for enjoyment. Here are some of the non-fiction texts you might come across:

CHINESE PUZZLE OVER WILLIAM THE FISH

WILLIAM the resident fish at Florence Fan's Chinese restaurant is a mouthy sort.

Whenever Florence, pictured above, approaches his tank he looks ready to bite her head off. And he's the same with her women customers – one gaze at a female and he goes into a rage, kicking up the sand in his aquarium.

But it's a different story when a man approaches his tank at a Birmingham restaurant. William, a giant gourami from South-East Asia, calms down and seems perfectly content, as though he were one of the lads.

Florence can't figure out the reason for his odd behaviour, but suspects he's just an old sexist with a sweet and sour personality.

Newspaper article

Advertisement

NSPCC

Cruelty to children must stop. FULL STOP.

National Society for the Prevention
of Cruelty to Children

42 Curtain Road
London EC2A 3NH
Telephone: 0171 825 2505

20th March 1999

Dear Supporter,

I am writing to you at a momentous time in our history.

The NSPCC is facing a greater challenge than any it has faced before, by launching a national campaign to *put a final full stop to child abuse*.

I hope we can count on you to help us, as you have so generously in the past. We cannot hope to succeed without the support of the general public:

Letter

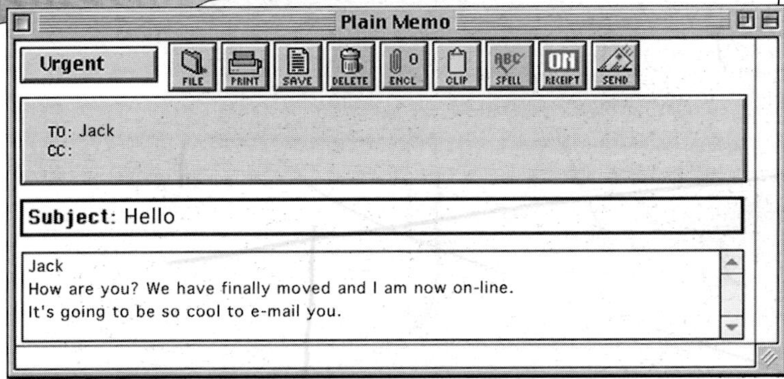

Plain Memo

Urgent | FILE | PRINT | SAVE | DELETE | ENCL | CLIP | SPELL | RECEIPT | SEND

TO: Jack
CC:

Subject: Hello

Jack
How are you? We have finally moved and I am now on-line.
It's going to be so cool to e-mail you.

E-mail to a friend

BEARS' BEANFEAST

Serves 4

INGREDIENTS
1 large onion
1 teaspoon corn oil
8 chipolata sausages
1×450 g (1 lb) can baked beans
75 g (3 oz) frozen mixed vegetables
2 slices processed Cheddar cheese

YOU WILL NEED
knife, for chopping
chopping board
teaspoon
frying pan
fish slice
plate
wooden spoon
can opener
tiny cocktail cutter

Preparation time: 15 minutes
Cooking time: 25 minutes

1. Peel and chop the onion and put it to one side.
2. Put the oil into a frying pan and heat it gently. Add the sausages and cook gently for about 10 minutes, turning frequently with a fish slice until the sausages are golden brown all over.
3. Transfer the sausages to a plate with the fish slice. Fry the chopped onion in the frying pan for 5 minutes, stirring often with the wooden spoon.
4. Carefully drain off the oil from the pan. Add the baked beans and frozen mixed vegetables and stir well.
5. Cook until the mixture is bubbling, then return the sausages to the pan and cook gently for 6 minutes, stirring occasionally.
6. Cut out small shapes from the cheese, using the tiny cutter, and arrange these on top of the mixture. Serve hot with chunks of crusty bread.

Recipe

Activity 1 ICT

1 What other kinds of non-fiction texts can you name? Make a list of them.

2 Think about the different types of non-fiction texts you have read in the past week. Copy and complete the following chart:

Type of text	Where I read it	What it was about

3 Make a list of the different types of non-fiction texts you might find in the following places:

◆ a train station ◆ a teenage magazine ◆ a school notice board.

Presenting information

In Year 7 you will come across many different types of non-fiction textbook, probably at least one for each subject you study. Each type presents information to you in a particular way, which will be affected by:

- the subject being studied
- the information being presented.

As you become more familiar with the different types of textbook, you will see similarities in the ways they present information. They will often use the same, or similar, presentational features. Writers use these to organize their information on the page and to draw the reader's attention to particular things.

Read the extract from a food technology textbook on the opposite page, and then complete the activity below.

Activity 2 WS ICT

1 The main presentational features have a letter beside them. Copy and complete the following chart by correctly matching the letter to the feature. The first one is done for you.

Presentational feature	Letter
unit number	D
title or heading	
sub-heading	
bold print	
bullet points	
illustrations	

2 Now think about *why* these particular features have been used. Match each feature to its possible purpose(s).

Purpose	Presentational feature
to divide the information up clearly	
to tell you what the chapter is about	
to tell you what a part of the chapter is about	
to organise a series of separate points	
to make the main points stand out	
to make it look more interesting	

D

6 Introducing Food

B

C

Food and You

Cars, like people, come in all shapes and sizes.

E

To function properly, cars need fuel. Fuel consists of a lot of petrol, a moderate amount of oil and a little grease.

People, too, need fuel to function. Our fuel needs are met by **food**.

Our fuel consists of:

F

- foods which we need the **most** of, such as bread, cereals, fruit and vegetables.

- foods that we need a **moderate** amount of, such as milk, cheese and yoghurt, meat, eggs and poultry, nuts and pulses.

A

- foods that we need the **least** of, such as butter, margarine, oil and sugar.

The following extract is taken from a geography textbook. Read it carefully and find these presentational features:

◆ heading ◆ sub-heading ◆ bold print ◆ photographs.

PLACES FOR PEOPLE

PLACE STUDY

Nottingham, UK, 2

In the present century large housing estates have been built on the edge of Nottingham. Old housing areas have been either improved, or demolished and rebuilt. Some old industries have moved out of the city to new sites where there is more space.

Population change

1901	239 700
1931	276 200
1961	311 900
1991*	273 000

Activity 3

1 A caption is a brief explanation which tells you something about a picture. Match these captions to the photographs in the extract:

- **i** Some old industries have moved to the edge of the city
- **ii** Twentieth-century houses south of the river
- **iii** Good access to Nottingham
- **iv** A re-developed housing area near the city centre

2 The chart gives you extra information. The information is presented in figures rather than words. Write down, in sentences, all the information you are given in this chart.

You could start your writing like this:

The population of Nottingham changed between nineteen hundred and one and nineteen hundred and ninety-one. In nineteen hundred and one the population was two hundred and thirty-nine thousand and seven hundred.

Why do you think the writer uses figures rather than words?

Charts, diagrams, drawings and photographs play an important part in the presentation of information. Sometimes, as you have just seen, a picture has a caption which helps to explain it. At other times writers use labels to tell you more about the picture. Read this extract from a science textbook about using bunsen burners:

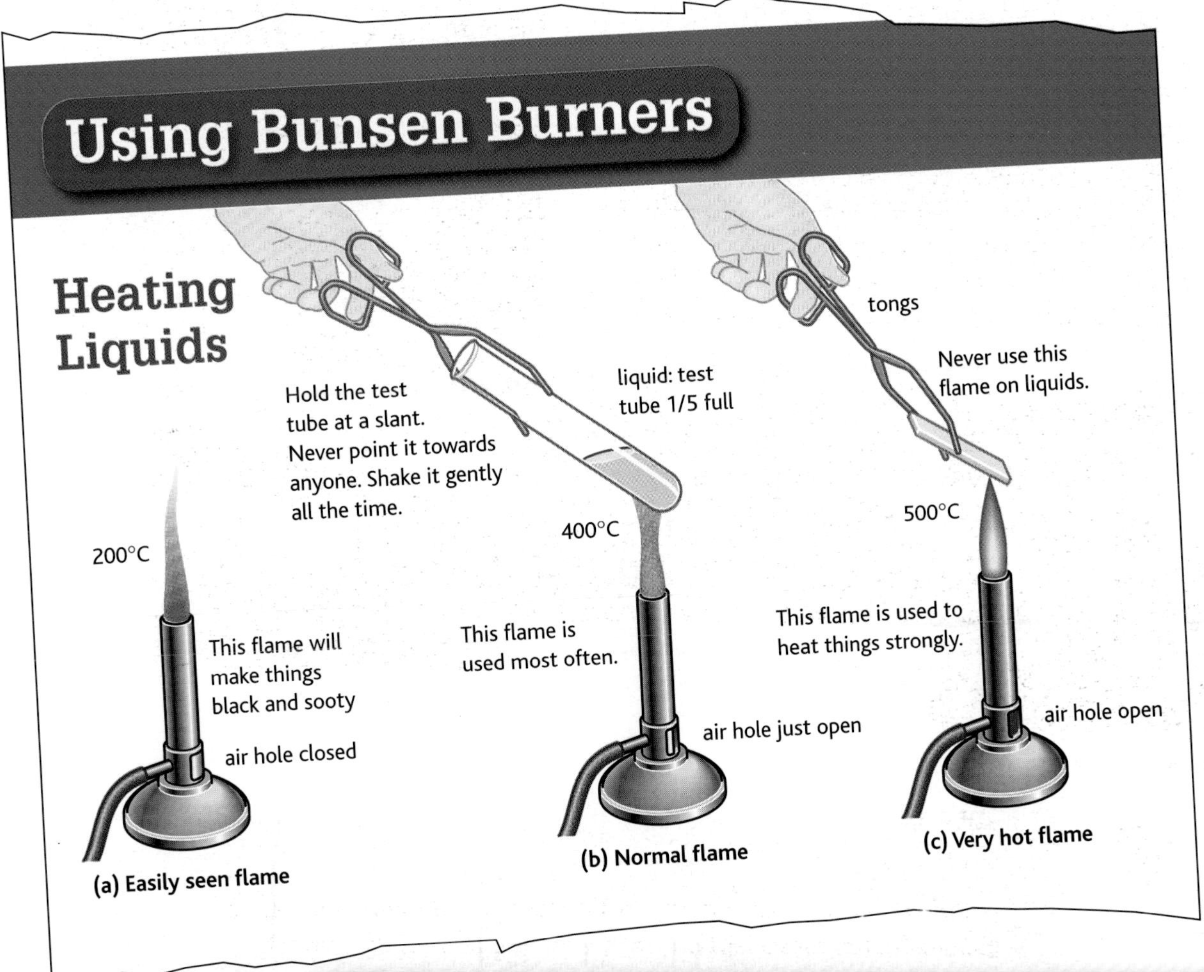
Using Bunsen Burners
Heating Liquids
Hold the test tube at a slant. Never point it towards anyone. Shake it gently all the time.
liquid: test tube 1/5 full
tongs
Never use this flame on liquids.
200°C
400°C
500°C
This flame will make things black and sooty
air hole closed
This flame is used most often.
air hole just open
This flame is used to heat things strongly.
air hole open
(a) Easily seen flame
(b) Normal flame
(c) Very hot flame

Activity 4 WS

1 What do you learn from the diagram and labels about the following:
   - **a** how to get different flames
   - **b** the temperature differences between the flames
   - **c** the effects of the different flames
   - **d** how to hold a test tube
   - **e** the things you should *not* do?

2 Suppose the writer had decided to explain all this information *without* using a labelled diagram. Try to write the explanation that would be needed.

3 What are the advantages of using a labelled diagram to explain this particular information?

Paragraphs

Writers use headings and sub-headings to help them organise their information. Another way of doing this is through the use of **paragraphs**. There are two ways of showing the reader where a new paragraph begins:

- by indenting the first word so that it starts a little way in from the margin
- by leaving a line space between two paragraphs.

The paragraph is a visual sign to the reader that something new is being introduced. Each paragraph has its own topic. It may link to the paragraphs before and after it, but it is possible to identify within it a new and different idea.

Activity 5 WS ICT

1 Look at the two extracts opposite. Read Text A about Viking children. In this text the paragraphs are indented.

Identify the main topic of each paragraph in Text A. The first one is done for you.

Paragraph 1 – *Viking children needed to be strong to survive.*

Notice how each paragraph has links with the one that follows it. The ideas are placed in a logical order, moving from death to survival and from babies to children.

2 Now read Text B. This text has been set out with a line space between each paragraph.
The paragraphs are not placed in their correct and logical order. Reorganise them in the correct order. Explain the order you have chosen.

Text A

Viking children were the pride of their parents. Because life was so hard, many children probably died before they reached adulthood. Those who did survive must have been very strong and independent.

Although there was an ancient law that allowed babies to be killed, this happened very rarely. Only those babies that were weak and did not look as if they could survive the rigours of Viking life, or babies born when there was a famine, were left outside to die.

Most new babies were welcomed into the family. They were given a name, sprinkled with water, and then lifted on to their father's knee as a sign of acceptance into the family. Children were given presents to mark the occasion, and later received another one when they cut their first tooth.

As soon as children were old enough, their parents began to teach them all they knew. Girls were taught how to spin and weave by their mothers, and boys went out in fishing boats with their fathers. Both worked on the family farm. They took the pigs to market, scared birds away from the crops, and helped at home with baking, smoking fish, making butter and many other household tasks.

As well as working hard, children found time to play. During the day, in the cold northern winters, they skated on icy ponds, wearing shoes with bone skates attached. We know they had balls and other wooden and fabric toys, although few of these have survived.

*from **The Vikings** by Anne Pearson*

Text B

a As time passed the kings grew more successful in controlling the chieftains. They took away many of the chieftains' powers and gradually unified their lands under royal sovereignty, or control.

b Viking society was clearly divided into classes. At the top of the social structure were the royal families. Viking kings were brave warriors who led their men in battle, and protected their people from pirates and invaders. They usually had the final say in matters of law, and they acted as religious leaders.

c Just below the kings were the chieftains or nobles, who were landowners and warriors. These were the fierce Vikings who raided abroad and led the armies that terrorised much of western Europe in the ninth and tenth centuries. In early Viking times, many powerful chieftains had their own large war bands and controlled vast areas of Scandinavia.

d The kings came from ancient royal families, but wealth and royal blood were not always enough to keep them in power. A new king also had to be declared the rightful ruler by his free subjects – though the support of the chieftains and reputation of his warriors could be very persuasive! A king who lost the support of his chieftains would be exiled or even killed. A cruel or unjust king could be legally overthrown.

Use of colour

As you have seen, drawings and photographs are often used in non-fiction texts to illustrate ideas and to add interest to the written material. Colours are used because they can have a strong impact and affect the way we respond to a text. We tend to link certain colours with particular moods and ideas. Take the colour black.

What do we mean if we say that someone is in a black mood?

Which of the following do you associate with the colour black?
◆ mystery ◆ darkness ◆ excitement ◆ jealousy
◆ death ◆ depression ◆ evil ◆ love ◆ hatred

Think about the following colours.
What moods and ideas do they suggest to you?

Look at the following leaflet fronts.
What do the colours suggest to you?

How are the colours linked to the subject of each leaflet?

Bringing it all together

Look at and read the following leaflet:

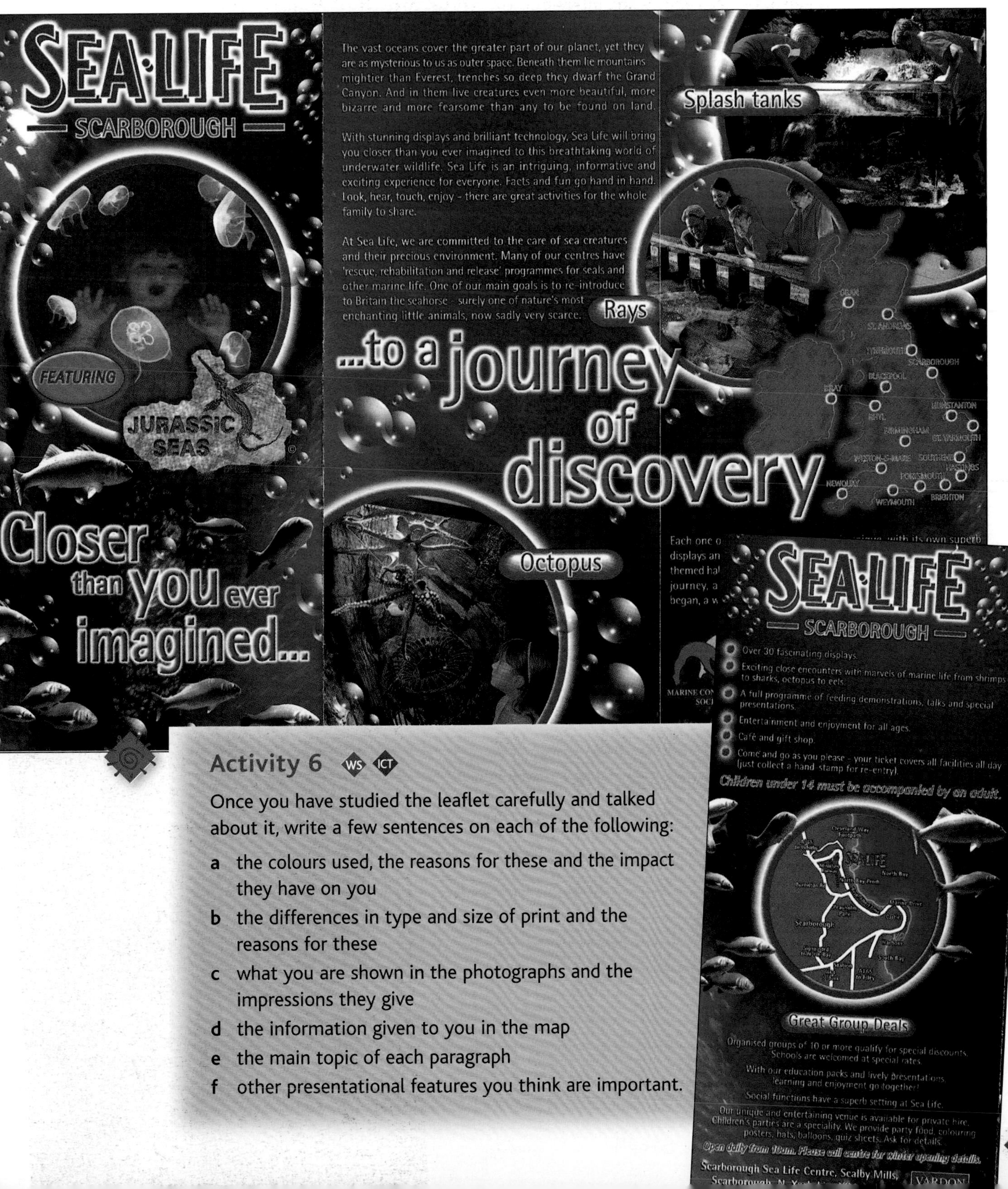

Activity 6

Once you have studied the leaflet carefully and talked about it, write a few sentences on each of the following:

- **a** the colours used, the reasons for these and the impact they have on you
- **b** the differences in type and size of print and the reasons for these
- **c** what you are shown in the photographs and the impressions they give
- **d** the information given to you in the map
- **e** the main topic of each paragraph
- **f** other presentational features you think are important.

6 Finding out about non-fiction

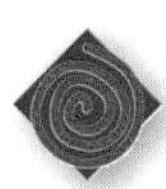

This unit will help you to:
- **identify features of different non-fiction texts**
- **recognise that all texts have a purpose**
- **recognise that all texts have an intended audience**
- **understand that choice of words is linked to purpose and audience**
- **understand the difference between fact and opinion.**

As you have seen, there are many different types of non-fiction texts. In just one day a person might:

- receive leaflets and letters in the post
- glance through the morning newspaper
- pass signs and adverts on the way to work
- read instructions, faxes and e-mails at work
- read a magazine on the way home
- access the Internet in the evening.

There are things you can learn about non-fiction texts which will help you to deal with this huge range of material which is part of daily life.

Form

Each type of non-fiction text has its own particular form. Form is the word we use to describe the way a text is set out on the page. It is often possible to recognise what kind of text you are looking at without even having to read it. How many of the following texts can you identify just by looking at them?

A

4 Branwell Close
Branwell
Herts
30th May, 2000

Dear Beth,

How are you? It seems ages since we last met up, even though it was only a couple of weeks ago.

The main reason I'm writing is to invite you to my birthday party. It's at my house on the 16th of June. All the gang are coming so we should have a great time. Please make sure you make it.

Hope everything's going well at the new school. We all miss you lots. Ring me as soon as you get this ... or else!

See you soon, (I hope)

Steph

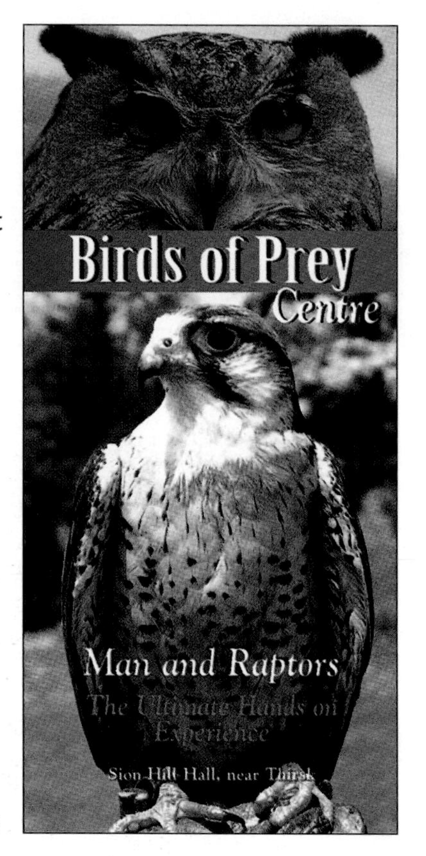

Birds of Prey
Centre
Man and Raptors
The Ultimate Hands on Experience

B

C

ENGLISH

Name : Jayne Marshall Year-group : 7

Form : IP Teaching-group : KR

NATIONAL CURRICULUM TEACHER ASSESSMENT

LEVEL RANGE	AT1	AT2	AT3
2 - 3			
3 - 5	✓	✓	✓
5 - 7			

ATTAINMENT TARGET 1 (AT1) : Speaking & Listening
ATTAINMENT TARGET 2 (AT2) : Reading
ATTAINMENT TARGET 3 (AT3) : Writing (including Handwriting, Spelling & Punctuation)

	Excellent	Good	Satisfactory	Poor	Unsatisfactory	Not applicable
Attitude/behaviour	✓					
Presentation of work		✓				
Oral skills			✓			
Effort		✓				
Working with others		✓				
Completion of homework		✓				

Teacher's comments :
Jayne works hard in class and is making good progress with her English studies.

D

LEEDS UNITED
FOOTBALL CLUB

Packard Bell. PUMA planetfootball.com

THE NEWS | THE SHOP | TEAM STATS | THE BUSINESS | THE CLUB | THE FANS | COMPS N CHAT | FEEDBACK

COMPETITION Welcome to Elland Road

15% off all available Puma merchandise

Winter Sale Specials !!!

LUFC TICKET OFFICE

LATEST NEWS HEADLINES

JUMPING JASON
United duo Nigel Martyn and Jason Wilcox have both been included in Kevin Keegan's England squad to play Argentina at Wembley next Wednesday........ More

YORKE U-TURN
Manchester United striker Dwight Yorke has been amazingly released by Trinidad and Tobago from their Gold Cup campaign and will fly back to England in time to face Leeds on Sunday........ More

HUCK HAPPY WITH BENCH-LIFE
United striker Darren Huckerby has insisted he has no complaints with life on the Leeds substitute bench, as long as........ More

UNITED CHAIRMAN IN TWO HORSE RACE
Leeds Chairman Peter Ridsdale is battling it out with Arsenal's David Dein to become the vice-chairman of the new FA's executive board........ More

FALL GUYS FACE INJURY CRISIS
United boss David O'Leary has claimed Leeds, Tottenham, Chelsea and Wimbledon are victims of a backlash from the FA, as he counts the walking wounded ahead of the Manchester United clash on Sunday............ More

UNITED FANCY THEIR CHANCES
Leeds keeper Nigel Martyn will have a simple message for his Leeds team mates on Sunday morning when Manchester United arrive at Elland Road........ More

WATCH OUT - HOPPY'S BACK
Leeds' Scottish midfielder David Hopkin is back and has promised United fans he'll be playing a key role for the Whites in the run in to the Premiership and UEFA Cup campaigns........ More

SUPER SIX
United have six players in the England U-21 squad for a friendly against Argentina at Fulham's Craven Cottage next week........ More

Activity 1 WS ICT

Here are some of the features that probably helped you to recognise that Text A is a letter:

- the address and date are set out separately
- the greeting, *Dear Beth*
- the use of paragraphs to organise the content
- the ending and signature, *See you soon, Steph.*

What features helped you to identify the other texts? List them.

Audience

All writers write for someone. The intended reader is called the **audience**. The audience may be one person, as in a letter to a friend, or many people, as in a letter to a magazine. Read Text A. Who do you think it was written for?

A

This is a robin.
A robin is a bird.
A bird can sing.
A robin is a songbird

Did you guess correctly? The text was written for young children, probably between four and six years old. There are several clues that give this away:

- the illustration is clear and bright
- the sentences are very short and simple
- the words are fairly easy to read
- the words are repeated to help the reader learn them.

This book, however, does have another audience. Who else will it need to appeal to? Who will probably buy it?

B

February 23 1827
To school in the morning where the usual routine of Spelling, Reading, Writing, Cyphering, Burching and Caneing took place.

March 6
To school: find it impossible to arrive there at the proper time owing to the long distance from home. This is a great drawback to my advancement in study.

March 10
Dragged along to school: George, Bridgman, Jennings, Kynaston, Hendry, Page are all beating me hollow at Latin. Really, I am quite discouraged.

April 2
In terrible agony with the toothache. Ran up the village almost mad to Dr Rogers, who could not extract it.

May 16
Papa dared me to have my tooth out, accordingly put my courage to the test and went with him to Hayes, the celebrated dentist in Bedford Court. My first impression when he pulled it out was that he had pulled my head off instead of the tooth.

Activity 2

Read Texts B, C and D. Try to identify their intended audiences. Once you have decided on the intended audience, talk about the reasons for your decision.

C

Booked: Gray, McIntyre. **Goals:** McIntyre 28, Caskey 73.

Wycombe: Taylor, Lawrence, Cousins, Ryan, Vinnicombe (McSporran 72), Carroll (Devine 65), Simpson, Emblen, Brown, Baird, Scott. Subs Not Used: McCarthy. **Booked:** Simpson, Emblen, Brown. **Goal:** Devine 80. **Att:** 10,298 **Ref:** P Danson (Leicester).

Stoke City (0) 2 Notts County (0) 3

Stoke: Ward, J. Kavanagh, Woods, Sigurdsson, Robinson, O'Connor, Keen, G. Kavanagh, Wallace, MacKenzie, Oldfield. Subs Not Used: Petty, Taaffe, Collins. **Goals:** Oldfield 68, Keen 90.

Notts County: Ward, Hendon, Pearce, Liburd, Dyer, Richardson, Creaney, Redmile, Stallard, Beadle (Rapley 59), Tierney. **Subs Not Used:** Holmes, Garcia. **Goals:** Beadle 54, Liburd 76, Stallard 85. **Att:** 9,565 **Ref:** G Gain (Bootle).

Shrewsbury (1) 2 Chester (0) 0

Shrewsbury: Edwards, Seabury, Wilding, Tretton, Herbert, Hanmer, Preece, Jobling, Berkley, Kerrigan (Brown 76), Steele. **Subs Not Used:** Craven, Jagielka. **Goals:** Steele 7, 88.

Chester: Brown, Davidson, Crosby, Aisford, Cross, Richardson, Flitcroft, Carson (Shelton 84), Smith, Murphy, Beckett. **Subs Not Used:** Lancaster, Wright. **Booked:** Davidson, Carson. **Att:** 2,903 **Ref:** K Lynch (Kirk Hammerton).

Swansea City (1) 1 Halifax (0) 2

Swansea: Freestone, O'Leary, Howard, Cusack, Smith, Bound, Roberts, Casey (Lacey 77), Alsop, Watkin, Coates. **Subs Not Used:** Bird, Jenkins. **Booked:** Casey. **Goal:** Cusack 17.

Halifax: Martin, J. Murphy, Bradshaw, Sertori, Stansfield (Paterson 61), Brown, O'Regan (Lucas 84), Hulme, Hanson, Butler, Power. **Subs Not Used:** S. Murphy. **Booked:** J. Murphy, O'Regan, Hulme. **Goals:** J. Murphy 77, Paterson 90. **Att:** 4,974 **Ref:** A. D'Urso (Billericay).

D

Purpose

All writing is written for a reason. Can you work out why Text E was written?

E

HOW TO PLAY

Pass the Bomb

by Gibsons Games

Aim of the Game

To make words which include the letters printed on the card before the bomb goes off!

Playing the Game

Shuffle the cards together, deal 13 cards into a pile, and put the rest to one side. The first players starts by taking the bomb and the die. Roll the die; this decides whereabouts in the word the letters may be used.

Letters may not be used at the start of the word

Letters may be used anywhere in the word

Letters may not be used at the end of the word

Now start the bomb, and quickly turn over the top card from the pile of 13. These are the letters which must be used until the bomb explodes. As soon as you have said a word which includes the letters, pass the bomb on to the player on your left. Play continues until the bomb goes off. Whoever has the bomb at that time is given the card that has been used as a penalty, and starts the next round by rolling the die, starting the bomb, and turning over the next card.

Did you guess correctly? These instructions were written to show you how to play a particular game.

When we talk about the reason behind a piece of writing, we call it the purpose. Just as a text can have more than one audience, it can also have more than one purpose.

Activity 3

Read Texts F, G and H on the opposite page. Try to work out the purpose(s) of each one. Once you have decided, talk about the reasons for your decisions.

F
Pearl
Altus
Sheehan's
Music Services
The Midlands Flute Specialist
Why travel further?
We have: • Specialist staff
• Large stocks of flutes and accessories
• Competitive prices
• Qualified and experienced repairers
50 London Road • Leicester LE2 OQD
Tel (0116) 255 7492 • Fax (0116) 285 59
Next to the railway station
JUPITER
SANKYO
TREVOR JAMES & Co
The Muramatsu flute
G
2 pts milk
pack of cornflakes
sugar
butter
soap
sliced loaf
choc. biscuits
ham
cheese
fruit juice.
H

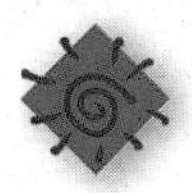

Activity 4 WS

Make a chart like the one below. Complete the Audience and Purpose columns for Texts A–H on pages 60–63. Text A has been done for you.

Text	Audience(s)	Purpose(s)
A	young child and parent	to give information about birds in an interesting way that a young child would understand
B		
C		

Formal and informal language

When you are talking to friends you probably speak in a different way from the way you speak to your teachers. You change the way you speak depending on who you are talking to and why you are talking to them.

In the first example the girl is using **informal speech**. In the second example the boy is using **formal speech**.

It is the same for writers. The way they write depends on the audience they are writing for and the purpose for which they are writing.

The following extract is a report for a school magazine about a school football match:

CONGRATULATIONS to the Year Seven Football Team who reached the county cup final last week, thanks largely to a late, but brilliant, two-goal salvo from striker Mark Smith. Unfortunately, the game was marred by an ugly incident after the final whistle, involving the opposition team's manager and the referee.

Our boys opened the scoring early on, with James Walker hitting a superb free kick after seven minutes to put his side 1–0 up. By half-time, however, he had been removed from the field for abusive language to an official.

In the second half, play swung from end to end, but Smith's two late goals were more than enough to claim a place in the final. Let us hope that the team can avenge last year's unfortunate defeat, and lift the trophy second time around.

Chris Harbron

The following extract is taken from a letter in which the same writer tells his friend about the same match:

... Talking about footy, you should have seen our school's cup match last week. It was absolutely class – four goals, a red card and a punch-up in the centre circle. The game had everything!

And Jimbo's goal – what a scorcher! It flew right into the top corner – the keeper had no chance. Then he got sent off for swearing at the linesman – but I reckon he was dead unlucky. Anyway, Smithy scored another two in injury time to win it – but their goal was miles offside – it should never have stood in the first place.

Then, right at the end, their P.E. teacher got really mad with the ref and ended up flooring him! It was brill! I can't wait for the next game, the cup final. With a bit of luck our lads won't get thrashed again like last year...

Chris Harbron

Activity 5 WS ICT

1 Which of these accounts uses language:
- formally
- informally?

2 Full names are given in the formal report. What nicknames are used to replace these in the letter?

3 In the report you will find the words *football*, *referee* and *brilliant*. What are the shortened informal forms of these in the letter?

4 'Slang' is a term used to describe informal language. An example of this in the letter is

It was absolutely class!

Write down any other examples you can find in the letter.

5 What differences can you find in the use of punctuation in the two accounts?

6 Choose something that you have watched recently. It could be a football match, your favourite TV soap, a film, a concert or something else.

Write part of a letter to a friend in which you tell him or her about it. Your purpose is to explain what happened and your thoughts about it. Use language informally.

Fact and opinion

A fact is something that can be proved to be true:

An earwig has six legs.

You can prove this by looking in an encyclopaedia or, easier still, by looking at an earwig. Therefore it is a fact.

An opinion is a statement of a point of view which cannot be proved or disproved:

Ladybirds are much nicer than earwigs.

This is based on an individual judgement. It can neither be proved or disproved. Therefore it is an opinion.

Activity 6 ICT

Below is a mixture of facts and opinions.

Using the letters next to the statements, make two lists, one of facts and one of opinions.

a Insects make brilliant pets.

b Ants can lift objects that weigh more than they do.

c Dung beetles are so named because they feed on animal droppings.

d Being stung by a wasp is more painful than having an injection.

e Flies are nothing but a nuisance.

f All worker ants are female.

g An insect begins life as an egg.

h Flies and mosquitoes carry some of the world's most serious diseases.

i The silkworm is the caterpillar of a moth.

j A spider's web is delicate and beautiful.

k Bees' honey tastes lovely.

l A bee's buzzing sound is made by the movement of its powerful wings.

m If I were an ant I'd go on strike.

n A flea can leap more than 30 cm up into the air.

o A ladybird will bring you good luck.

p A honeybee colony may contain 50,000 bees.

When you have finished, check your lists with a friend. Were there any statements you weren't sure about? What helped you to decide whether they were facts or opinions?

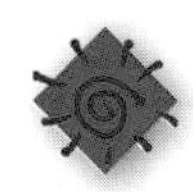

Activity 7

Read the following comments about spiders. Which are facts and which are opinions?

A spider has two parts to its body. It has eight legs and usually has eight eyes. Many spiders capture insects by spinning a silken web. They can run up walls and along ceilings because they have claws and pads on their legs. Many people call spiders insects but they really belong to a group of animals called arachnids.

I think spiders are fantastic creatures. They look so fierce and almost evil and yet really I don't think they'd harm you. Their webs are fascinating. It's really clever the way they seem to take ages making them and then just hang around for something to come along. None of the other insects have got a chance against the spider.

Activity 8 WS ICT

Now try it yourself.
What facts might the scientist give about this butterfly?
What opinions might the schoolboy have?
Use the picture to help you.

7 Reading for different purposes

This unit will help you to:
- develop skills in scanning a text
- develop skills in skim reading
- identify key points in a text
- increase awareness of implicit meaning
- draw conclusions with caution.

Scanning

When you are looking for information in an encyclopaedia or reference book you usually first turn to the index at the back. The index tells you what page or pages you need to turn to in order to find the particular topic you are looking for. Your eyes move quickly over the surface until you see the topic you want. This type of reading is called **scanning**.

Here is part of an index taken from a book on UFOs.

In order to use an index quickly and accurately there are a few things you need to know:

- All the entries are in alphabetical order.
- Names of people are indexed by surname rather than first name or title.
- Some entries have more than one page reference and you need to look briefly at each to find the information you want.
- Many words and phrases have 'The' placed before them, e.g. *The Milky Way*. They are indexed by the first word to follow 'The', i.e. *Milky*.

Activity 1

Using the index, see how quickly you can find the page references for the following:

Rex Pixley	fake photographs	the Moon
UFO sightings	Manuel Perez	John Young
radio telescopes	the origins of life	meteoroids

Once you have found the page you want you still may not need to read it all. Often you need to scan it to find the information you want. You know the key words you are looking for and you scan the page until you find them. Only then do you stop and actually read.

Activity 2

Scan the following text to see how quickly you can find the answers to these questions:

1 How many ships have disappeared in The Bermuda Triangle?
2 What have the stars got to do with the pyramids?
3 What country is near The Bermuda Triangle?
4 When were the pyramids built?
5 What do some experts say the lines on the Nazca Plateau look like?
6 What has been found of the ships lost in The Bermuda Triangle?

Unsolved puzzles

UFOs are not a new phenomenon. People have been spotting them in the skies for centuries, but until newspapers and television spread information, few people knew about them. According to some researchers, UFOs even visited some of man's earliest civilisations. See what you think.

Help from space?

The pyramids in Egypt were built more than 3,000 years ago, using only very simple tools. They are such an amazing feat of building that some people cannot believe that the Egyptians built them on their own. Did they have help from an alien civilisation with technical knowledge far superior to theirs?

There's no evidence to prove this theory, but the pyramids are the source of many unanswered questions . . .

Star power

One mystery surrounds the way the pyramids seem to line up so precisely with some of the stars in the night sky. Can this be just a coincidence, or were the stars especially important to the pyramid builders for some reason?

Dangerous waters

Far more menacing is one theory behind the mysterious disappearance of 120 ships and planes while crossing a triangular area of open sea near the island of Bermuda. The 'jinxed' area is now known as The Bermuda Triangle. Among possible explanations for the disappearances is that aliens are 'beaming up' ships and planes to join them in space, so that they can find out about life on Earth.

Space signs

The Nazca Plateau in Peru, South America, is the site of another possible UFO puzzle. Broad, long lines and huge animal shapes were cut into rock 1,500 years ago by Indian tribes.

Some experts argue that the lines look like a massive airstrip for UFOs. Did the Indians carve the shapes to show passing aliens what lives on this planet?

Crop circles

In 1980, reports began coming in about circular patches of grain in English fields being mysteriously flattened. As more flat 'crop circles' were found, some argued they were caused by flying saucers landing in the fields.

Skimming

When we scan a text, we are looking for a particular area we want to read more carefully. Sometimes, however, we may want to read the whole of a text quickly in order to get a general idea of what it is about. This will then tell us whether we need to read it more carefully or whether we can move on to the next page. This type of reading is called **skimming**.

Give yourself one minute to skim this text.

CLOSE ENCOUNTERS

A recent survey in America revealed that 26 per cent of Americans believe that they have seen an Unidentified Flying Object (UFO). That is 90 million people. Thousands of people claim to have been actually abducted by aliens. By this they mean they have been kidnapped and taken on board flying saucers. So can you really be sure it won't happen to you?

If you do come across an alien, it is known as a close encounter. If you just see a UFO it is called a close encounter of the first kind. If the UFO leaves a mark, like a burn on the ground, it is an encounter of the second kind. In an encounter of the third kind, you actually meet an alien. The fourth, and most scary kind, is alien abduction.

Fact or fiction? Thousands of UFO sightings are reported every year. Many are studied by enthusiasts called UFOlogists. They spend their time searching for evidence of extra-terrestrial life, which means life beyond our planet.

Most sightings turn out to be nothing more than an aircraft, the Moon, or weather balloons. But, to this day, over 200,000 sightings remain unexplained, and the witnesses involved remain convinced that they have encountered aliens. Some people think that the kind of person who sees a UFO has an over-active imagination, but can so many people be mistaken?

Case studies This book contains eight case studies. In each study there is an account of a famous close encounter based on eye witness reports. Each account is followed by an assessment, in which the facts of the story are examined in an attempt to discover what really happened.

Don't panic It is very hard to prove conclusively whether aliens are invading our planet. In the end, it is up to you to decide what you believe. If, when you have read this book, you feel that there is strong evidence to suggest that aliens do actually exist – don't panic. If they are here, they have probably been visiting our planet for centuries, and they haven't harmed us yet.

Activity 3

Find out how well you have skim-read the passage. Can you point to the parts of the text that would give you the answers to the following questions?

1 What percentage of Americans believe they have seen a UFO?
2 What is a close encounter of the third kind?
3 What do we call people who study UFO sightings?
4 What is meant by extra-terrestrial life?
5 How many sightings remain unexplained?
6 What is the rest of the book about?

The ability to skim-read is an important skill which improves with practice. Set yourself time targets and, once you've reached them, try to improve on them. Remember your aim in skim-reading is to get a general understanding of a text.

Reading for detail

So far we have looked at the ways you might read a text quickly, either to find out specific information or to get a general idea about something. Often, though, you do need to read a text carefully and in detail.

Identifying the key points

The first thing you need to be able to do when reading carefully is to follow what is happening. In order to do this, you need to identify the key points of a text.

As you have seen in unit 5, each paragraph has its own topic. You can use the paragraphs to help you identify the key points. Read this text on the sighting of a UFO.

Case study five: ALIENS IN THE DESERT

Date: July 2nd, 1947
Time: 9:50pm
Place: The Foster Ranch, near Corona, New Mexico, USA
Witness: Multiple witnesses

THE EVENTS

An ear-splitting explosion rang out across the desert. Just thunder, thought sheep rancher Mac Brazel, as he stood on the porch of the Foster Ranch. Yet he still felt uneasy as he watched the stormy night sky.

The next day, Mac rode out to check on his flock. As he paused at the top of a hill to wipe the sweat from his forehead, he suddenly noticed below him something glittering in the sunlight. A trail of wreckage littered the valley floor. It looked like the remains of a plane.

Gossip in town

Three days later, Mac went into the town of Corona for a drink. In the bar, he heard some customers talking about UFOs. Apparently several local people had reported seeing mysterious objects speeding across the sky. Mac wondered whether the strange debris he had found in the desert might be a UFO. He decided to go to the Sheriff's office to report his findings.

So far you have read the small box of factual details and three paragraphs.

The key points from the box are:

◆ 2 July, 1947 – 9.50pm – Corona, New Mexico, USA

The key points from each of the paragraphs are:

◆ paragraph 1 – Mac Brazel, a sheep rancher, heard an ear-splitting explosion.
◆ paragraph 2 – The next day he found what appeared to be the remains of a plane.
◆ paragraph 3 – Three days later Brazel reported his findings to the Sheriff.

Now read the rest of the extract on the next page.
For each paragraph that follows, write one sentence which sums up its key point.

Major Marcel investigates

The Sheriff rang Roswell Airbase, which immediately sent an Intelligence Officer named Major Jesse Marcel to go into the desert with Mac and investigate the wreckage.

What Major Marcel found was unlike anything he had ever seen before. Kneeling on the sand, he examined pieces of the debris. They appeared to be made of some kind of very light metal, like foil. There were little rods with symbols on them. When Jesse tested the debris, he found it couldn't be cut or burned. If he crumpled it up, it returned to its original shape.

Another strange discovery

Meanwhile, 290km (180 miles) southeast, Grady Barnett stood rigid with terror. While working in the desert, Barnett had come across a strange disc-shaped aircraft that had crashed into a hillside. Strewn around the craft were the bodies of its crew. He moved closer to get a better look. But what he saw made him freeze with horror.

A strange crew

The four bodies were abnormally thin, with big hairless heads, large eyes and small, slit-like mouths. They were only 1.4m (4ft 6in) tall, their arms were long and their hands had only four fingers. They were definitely not human.

Enter the army

Before Barnett could explore further, a US Army jeep roared up and a troop of soldiers descended on the crash site. They had been alerted by a pilot who had seen the damaged saucer from the air. One officer told Barnett to leave immediately and to tell no one about what he had seen. The soldiers sealed off the area until they had removed every trace of the debris.

That night, transporter planes flew out of Roswell Airbase under heavy guard, taking the crash wreckage to Wright-Patterson Airbase in Ohio.

Alerting the press

At noon the next day, an Information Officer at Roswell Airbase issued a statement which sent local newspapers crazy with excitement: a flying saucer had been found in the desert outside Corona.

Hours later, the airbase issued a new statement. The saucer story was a mistake. The crash debris was only a weather balloon. Reporters were invited to examine the fragments.

Held in isolation

Meanwhile, soldiers were sent to take Mac Brazel into custody. He was held in isolation, safely kept away from press reporters. The only statement he was allowed to make was to confirm the Army's new story.

Nobody knows what threats were made to ensure Mac never talked of what he had seen in the desert. But after his release, he didn't even discuss it with the members of his own family.

Activity 4 ◆ WS

Identifying the key points is an essential part of close and careful reading. Now that you have identified the key points of each paragraph, you should have a skeleton outline of the series of events. Check your outline with that of a friend. Are you missing any key points?

Implications

Writers choose their words carefully. Often they are trying to influence the way the reader thinks. They may suggest or imply certain things without saying them directly. When reading a text closely you need to be aware of what is being implied. Look at the following sentence:

Several local people had reported seeing mysterious objects speeding across the sky.

This sentence tells you the fact that other people had also seen strange things. This is not, however, the sentence the writer writes. She says: Apparently several local people had reported seeing mysterious objects speeding across the sky.

The word 'apparently' is used deliberately to suggest that this may not be a fact and that there is no real evidence for this. It is a warning to the reader to be careful.

Activity 5

Read the following sentences carefully. What is implied by them?

- **a** What Major Marcel found was unlike anything he had ever seen before.
- **b** They were definitely not human.
- **c** One officer told Barnett to leave immediately and to tell no one what he had seen.
- **d** That night transporter planes flew out of Roswell Airbase under heavy guard, taking the crash wreckage to Wright-Patterson Airbase in Ohio.

Conclusions

In reading, we draw conclusions on the basis of what we have read. This means that we weigh up the details that have been given to us and use them to help us make a judgement or arrive at a decision.

Activity 6

What do you think happened on 2 July 1947 in New Mexico? Answer these questions *and* give reasons for your answers.

1. What do you think Mac Brazel found in the desert?
2. What kind of metal did Major Marcel find?
3. Whose bodies were found by Grady Barnett?
4. Why was Barnett told to talk to no one about what he had seen?
5. Why did Roswell Airbase change its story about what had been found?

Knowing the whole picture

The problem with drawing conclusions is that we don't always have the whole picture. We are often only given part of the story. The following page of text gives you additional information that you didn't have before. Read it carefully:

Case study five: THE ASSESSMENT

The Roswell incident, as it is now known, is probably the best known UFO story. Countless wild claims have been made about what really happened.

Project Mogul

In 1994, the Air Force admitted that the balloon fragments shown to reporters at the press conference in 1947 were not the pieces of debris found outside Corona. The fragments the reporters were allowed to examine were from a Rawin Sonde balloon, which was a weather balloon. They claimed that the debris found outside Corona was from a Project Mogul balloon. Project Mogul balloons were designed to carry metal 'listening'discs that were being used to spy on the Soviet Union.

Top-secret tests

It seems probable that what crashed in the desert was a top-secret device that was being tested by the government. Scientists at White Sands missile range, near Roswell, were testing thousands of pieces of military equipment at this time.

Mystery material

Investigators believe that the strange metallic material that had so puzzled Major Marcel when he examined it may have been an early form of polyethylene. Polyethylene had indeed been invented in 1947, and it would have behaved in the manner Marcel described in his tests.

Nuclear weapons

In 1947, the airbase at Roswell was the home base for the world's only airborne combat unit trained to handle and drop nuclear bombs. Therefore, the transport planes seen secretly leaving the airbase under heavy guard on the night of July 8th, were more likely to have contained nuclear weapons than the remains of an alien saucer.

Crash test dummies

On June 24th, 1997, fifty years after the Roswell Incident, the United States Air Force revealed that during the 1940s, experiments were conducted in the area. Crash test dummies were thrown from high altitude research balloons. This might explain the 'aliens' seen in the desert by Grady Barnett.

Activity 7 WS

Look back at your answers to the questions in Activity 6. Are there any you would now change in the light of this new information? Write down which answers you would change and your reasons for changing them.

Read the following non-fiction text, then answer the questions overleaf.

THE WORLD / TODAY

The man who took on Jaws.. and survived

Lucky to be alive: Andrew Carter with the board he was riding when the great white shark struck in an attack which killed his tragic surfing pal off the coast of South Africa

Andrew back in the swim

BRAVE surfer Andrew Carter displays horrific wounds inflicted by a great white shark.

Beside him rests the bloodied and chewed board he keeps as a reminder of the day he cheated death.

And yesterday, Andrew plucked up courage to venture in the waves again.

It was the first time he had done so since his left leg was almost bitten off by the shark - immortalised in the Jaws films - off South Africa.

Attacked

Doctors had told him that he might never walk again, let alone surf.

Andrew, 32, was determined to prove them wrong.

But he chose less hazardous waters yesterday - at Newquay, Cornwall.

He joked: "I may catch my death of cold here but at least I won't get attacked by a shark. I thought I would never go back in the water again but surfing is my life."

He recalled that he survived the attack because a wave swept him to safety as the 15ft man-eater relaxed his bite to get a better grip.

But then the creature turned and tore at his pal, Bruce Corby, a 22-year-old student, who died a few hours later.

Andrew still gets panicky about the ordeal and has taken nearly a year to recover from his injuries.

Surgeons spent five hours re-constructing his leg with surgery involving hundreds of stitches. Now he has emigrated to England to get over the trauma and works in a Newquay surf shop. Reliving the shark attack, he said: "It had my leg and board in its jaws and was trying to bite through.

"Somehow it loosened its jaws and I slid away.

"I swam for the shore and looked back as the shark was thrashing around and chomping my board.

Victim

"It chased me but couldn't catch me so it went after Bruce and took his leg off with one bite."

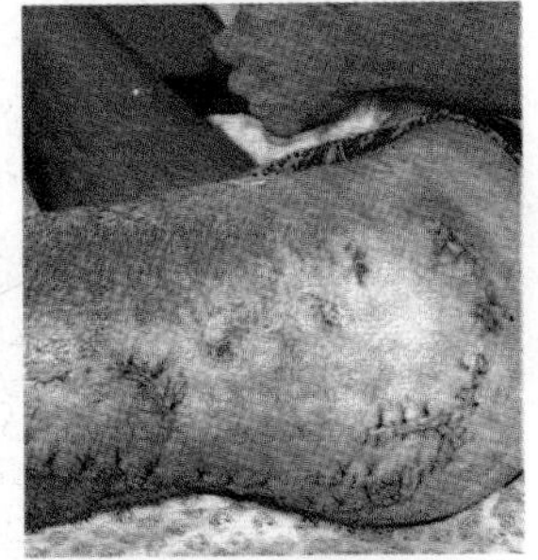

Bearing the scars: Stitches show where surgeons rebuilt Andrew's leg in five hours of surgery

A great white claimed its third victim in two weeks off Hong Kong yesterday.

The creature killed a 45-year-old woman swimmer.

Experts believe the shark could be responsible for other fatal attacks in the area in recent years.

1 What kind of non-fiction text is it? How do you know? List the features that helped you to recognise it.

2 Can you pick out the headings and sub-headings? Write them down.

3 You are given three pictures, two of which have captions.

   a What do the pictures show you?

   b Do the captions give you any extra information?

   c What difference would it make if the pictures were in black and white?

4 Who is the intended audience of this text? What is its intended purpose?

5 In the article the sequence of events is mixed up. Can you work out what happened in the correct order? The first point is:

   Nearly a year before Andrew and his friend, Bruce Corby, had been surfing off the coast of South Africa.

THE WORLD / TODAY

The man who took on Jaws.. and survived

Section B ◆ Writing
Introduction

Writing and reading are closely linked. If you are going to read something then someone has to write it first. The only reason for writing something has to be for someone – perhaps only yourself – to read it.

That's why, at the heart of learning to become a better writer, the ideas of *audience* and *purpose* are so important.

Audience matters. You've only got to think about the difference between a children's picture book and an adult's novel. One is quite short, written in short sentences with lots of pictures. The other is often hundreds of pages long with complicated sentences and demanding vocabulary. They are different because they are intended for different audiences.

The two books are very different, but both are intended to be read for pleasure. In that sense their *purpose* is the same. There are lots of other purposes for writing: people write to inform, to persuade, to organise thinking, to remember and for many other reasons.

For the purposes of this book, Creative Writing is a label for the writing of fiction, poems and plays and Non-fiction Writing covers a wide range of writing from posters to e-mails.

Computers have changed some approaches to writing. Most professional writing these days is done on a word-processor. So is a lot of writing in schools and at home. We hope that, as you work through the activities in this book, you will have access to a computer. Certain aspects of writing, such as drafting, are made much easier if you can use a word-processor. But handwriting is still very important: most people, however hi-tech their lives are, find themselves writing something by hand every day.

B1 Creative writing

Most writing is creative. We start with a blank piece of paper and we create some form of sense on it. A scientist doodling ideas on the back of an envelope, a copywriter in an advertising agency, someone writing a 'thank you' letter – all of these writers are being creative.

The name creative writing is used in this book to cover the kinds of writing associated with the imagination and making things up, like creating new worlds in stories, plays and poems.

The main purposes of these kinds of writing are to entertain and explore ideas. Stories, which are at the heart of fiction and drama, have always played a very important part in people's lives.

There are three units of work in this section.

The first unit, *Creating a sense of place*, focuses on descriptive writing. This is because description is an important aspect of story writing which is often neglected by young writers who are more concerned with 'getting on with' the plot rather than establishing a setting.

The focus of the second unit, *Different voices*, is on dialogue and playscripts. By working through the unit you should develop your ability to capture the different ways people talk.

The third unit, *Playing with words*, focuses on poetry and, in particular, how to make connections between words, ideas and sounds.

9 Creating a sense of place

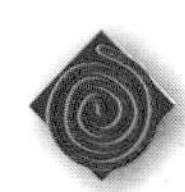

This unit will help you to:

- write better descriptions
- use vocabulary carefully and imaginatively
- learn about the importance of drafting.

Descriptive writing in prose

How you tell a story depends on who you're talking to or writing for – the audience. For example, if you were telling your friends a story about a particular teacher you all knew, you wouldn't need to describe the teacher or explain what he or she was like because your audience would know that already. But if you were telling the same story to someone who didn't know the school or the teacher you would need to give a bit of background information.

Writing descriptions is an important skill to develop. It helps your readers to 'see' something that you want to tell them.

Creating an impression

We often see descriptions of places. Some examples are:

- postcards when we write about where we're staying on holiday
- estate agents' descriptions of houses.

What other descriptions of places can you think of?

Sarah,
I'm having a really lovely time. It rained on the first day but since then the weather has been really hot and sunny. I've got my own room in the hotel and can see the sea from my window. The beach is lovely. The sand is white and the sea a beautiful shade of blue. I'd love to live somewhere like this.
Wish you were here! Claire

Sarah Madeley
32 Yew Tree Drive
Coventry
England

Number 15 Rose Lane is a beautifully situated semi-detached property with front and back landscaped gardens. It was built in 1932 and has been tastefully ...

In this section you are going to look at the kind of description you get in stories. Can you think of reasons why description in stories is important?

Describing a place to someone would be quite easy if you could give them a photograph. It's more difficult in words.

Look at the following photograph. It is from a postcard.

Activity 1 ICT

1 Look carefully at the postcard for a few moments. What do you think are the most striking features of the place? Make a list of them.

2 Now look at the postcard again. What can you see on a closer look that you *didn't* include in your first list? Add them to your list.

3 In pairs, compare your lists. You'll probably find that there are things you both missed.

4 There are some things that words can do better than a photograph. Imagine yourself into that postcard.

   a What kind of things do you think you could hear? List them.

   b What smells might there be? List them.

5 Write a description of the place in the postcard. Use your lists of sights, sounds, and smells as a starting point. Don't write too much: 8–12 lines will do. Before you write, think about the following:

   a Do you want your reader to like or dislike the place?

   b Which details in your list should you include and which should you leave out ?

Point of view

A photographer has to decide where to take a photograph from. With words you are not tied down to one particular point of view. When you describe something, it can be more like using a video camera which can move around until it dwells on one detail. The one final detail can seem important. Read the following extract:

Tuck Everlasting

She was unprepared for the homely little house beside the pond, unprepared for the gentle eddies of dust, the silver cobwebs, the mouse who lived – and welcome to him! – in a table drawer. There were only three rooms. The kitchen came first, with an open cabinet where dishes
5 were stacked in perilous towers without the least regard for their varying dimensions. There was an enormous black stove, and a metal sink, and every surface, every wall, was piled and strewn and hung with everything imaginable, from onions to lanterns to wooden spoons to washtubs. And in a corner stood
10 Tuck's forgotten shotgun.

*from **Tuck Everlasting** by Natalie Babbitt*

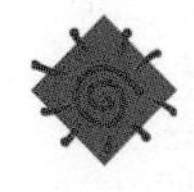

Activity 2 WS

1 What makes the detail of the shotgun stand out?

2 Imagine you have visited a friend's house for the first time. Describe their room. Build up the description like Natalie Babbitt does, so that you end by focusing on something interesting or strange.

Zooming in

When you describe something, you have to decide where to begin and end your description. One way to do this is to imagine you are filming a scene and zooming in. You may know the following text which has been taken from a children's picture book, written by Ruth Brown. It uses this idea:

Once upon a time there
was a dark, dark moor.

On the moor there was
a dark, dark wood.

5 In the wood there was
a dark, dark house.

At the front of the house
there was a dark, dark door.

Behind the door there
10 was a dark, dark hall.

In the hall there were
some dark, dark stairs.

Up the stairs there was
a dark, dark passage.

15 Across the passage was
a dark, dark curtain.

Behind the curtain was
a dark, dark room.

In the room was
20 a dark, dark cupboard.

In the cupboard was
a dark, dark corner.

In the corner was
a dark, dark box.

25 And in the box there
was … A MOUSE!

*from **Dark, Dark Tale***
by Ruth Brown

Beginning with a wide view and working up to one important detail can be very effective. It can help you plan an approach to description.

Activity 3 ICT

Look carefully at the pictures.
Imagine you are going to write a ghost or horror story. It's going to take place in the cellar of a house. Use the pictures to help you write your opening paragraph. Use two or three sentences for each picture, but only one sentence for the final one.

The walking shot

Sometimes it's best to put yourself in the scene and move around. The following extract is from *Skellig* by David Almond. Michael has just moved house and is exploring the garage:

Skellig

Something little and black scuttled across the floor. The door creaked and cracked for a moment before it was still. Dust poured through the torch beam. Something scratched and scratched in a corner. I tiptoed further in and felt spider webs breaking on my brow. Everything was packed in
5 tight – ancient furniture, kitchen units, rolled-up carpets, pipes and crates and planks. I kept ducking down under the hose-pipes and ropes and kitbags that hung from the roof. More cobwebs snapped on my clothes and skin. The floor was broken and crumbly. I opened a cupboard an inch, shone the torch in and saw a million woodlice scattering away. I
10 peered down into a great stone jar and saw the bones of some little animal that had died in there. Dead bluebottles were everywhere. There were ancient newspapers and magazines. I shone the torch on to one and saw that it came from nearly fifty years ago. I moved so carefully. I was scared every moment that the whole thing was going to collapse.
15 There was dust clogging my throat and nose. I knew they'd be yelling for me soon and I knew I'd better get out. I leaned across a heap of tea chests and shone the torch into the space behind and that's when I saw him.

from ***Skellig*** *by David Almond*

Activity 4 ICT

We see and hear and feel things as Michael moves around.

1 List the things Michael:
   a sees
   b hears
   c feels.

2 Think carefully about the description you have read and the kind of atmosphere the writer has created. Who do you think the 'him' is that Michael sees at the end of the paragraph?

Look at the following pictures. Imagine yourself walking around in one of those scenes.

Activity 5

Choose one of the pictures above. Write a description based on your chosen place that, like the extract from *Skellig*, ends with 'and that's when I saw him'.

The importance of details

When you write a story, you might want to concentrate on the action – what happens. After all, when you watch films you're mainly interested in the story. But in films you can always see the setting because it is there in the background. In stories, you have to put this background into words. Let's imagine you are going to write a story which begins with a new student arriving at your school, and coming into your classroom. It is their first day, they are nervous. As they glance around the room, what might they notice?

Activity 6 WS

1. List five things you think a new student might notice. Think about noises and even smells (chalk? disinfectant?) as well as sights.
2. Compare your list with a partner's. Explain to each other the reasons for your five choices. Make any changes you want to make to your list.
3. When you have finalised your list, use your five details to write a description of your classroom from the point of view of a newcomer. Begin like this:
   'The teacher opened the door and I took a step into the room ...'

Choosing effective details

It would be impossible to describe everything in a scene. You need to select the details that are important. What is important will depend on the kind of writing. Read the following extract:

Granny was a Buffer Girl

The Cutlers' Hall
was in Church Street,
near the middle of town.
Lights blazed from all its
5 windows. Even from the street
outside, with all its bustle of
trams and traffic, you could hear
the strains of the orchestra, and
the babble of voices and laughter.
10 Dorothy, shy, held on to her sister's
arm as they went up the steps to
the entrance hall. She gazed round
at the black and green walls that
gleamed like marble, the crystal
15 chandeliers, the glowing polish
of the woodwork; at the height
of the pillars and the decorated
ceiling, and at the
broad sweep of the
20 grand staircase that
she was going to
have to climb up if
she was ever going
to get near the
25 ballroom.

from Granny was a Buffer Girl by Berlie Doherty

Activity 7

Why do you think the writer chose to describe the details that are underlined in the text? What impression of the Hall is being made on Dorothy?

Using details to create atmosphere

Creative writing isn't just about describing things like people and objects. It can also describe moods or feelings. This can be called atmosphere. Read the two following extracts:

A I emerged into a small burial ground. It was enclosed by the remains of a wall, and I stopped in astonishment at the sight. There were perhaps fifty old gravestones, most of them leaning over or completely fallen, covered in patches of greenish-yellow lichen and moss, scoured pale by the salt wind, and stained by years of driven rain. The mounds were grassy, and weed-covered, or else they had disappeared altogether, sunken and slipped down. No names or dates were now decipherable, and the whole place had a decayed and abandoned air.

Ahead, where the wall ended in a heap of dust and rubble, lay the grey water of the estuary. As I stood, wondering, the last light went from the sun, and the wind rose in a gust, and rustled through the grass. Above my head, that unpleasant, snake-necked bird came gliding back towards the ruins, and I saw that its beak was hooked around a fish that writhed and struggled helplessly. I watched the creature alight and, as it did so, it disturbed some of the stones, which toppled and fell out of sight somewhere.

from ***The Woman in Black*** *by Susan Hill*

B The sun was up over the hills now and the mist had cleared and it was wonderful to be striding along the road with the dog in the early morning, especially when it was autumn, with the leaves changing to gold and yellow and sometimes one of them breaking away and falling slowly over in the air, dropping noiselessly right in front of him on to the grass beside the road. There was a small wind up above, and he could hear the beeches rustling and murmuring like a crowd of people.

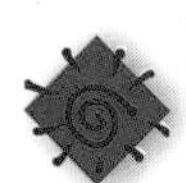

Activity 8 ◆ ICT

1. What is the difference in atmosphere between the two passages? Choose the best word to describe the atmosphere in each extract.
2. Once you have decided on your words, support your choices with three or four words or details from each extract.
3. Rewrite the second passage, changing some words and phrases to turn it into the beginning of a ghost story or a horror story.

Choosing your words carefully

Thinking about detail is only one part of writing interesting descriptions. You have to try to use language in interesting ways too. Your choice of words will depend on your purpose. Read the following two descriptions of strange creatures:

> Jack found it in the garden, early one morning when the day is new and life itself is being reborn. At first he thought it was an ordinary caterpillar, until it looked at him with a tiny, green, human face.
>
> No, he hadn't imagined the phenomenon. It was a caterpillar with a minute human head, bald as a baby's or an old man's. It had no eyebrows or eyelashes but a few little whiskers on its chin. White whiskers. Its eyes were jade green, bright and intelligent. The skin of its face was as green as its caterpillar body. With a pin, Jack gently prised open its minuscule mouth. It had tiny, tiny brilliantly green teeth.

from ***The Green Thing*** *by Rosemary Timperley*

> I beheld the wretch – the miserable monster whom I had created. He held up the curtain of the bed; and his eyes, if eyes they may be called, were fixed on me. His jaws opened, and he muttered some inarticulate sounds, while a grin wrinkled his cheeks. He might have spoken, but I did not hear; one hand was stretched out, seemingly to detain me, but I escaped, and rushed down stairs.

from ***Frankenstein*** *by Mary Shelley*

Word bank

phenomenon – remarkable thing
minuscule – tiny
inarticulate – wordless
detain – keep back

Activity 9

1 Although it is clearly a very strange creature, the caterpillar in the first extract is not at all frightening.

- a What details of the description support this point of view?
- b Which words and phrases make the creature seem harmless?

2 In the second description there are fewer details of the appearance of the monster.

- a How does that help to make it more frightening?
- b Which words and phrases make the creature seem threatening?

Activity 10 WS

Choose an animal, such as a cat or a dog. Write a description of it which makes it seem one of the following:

◆ frightening ◆ mysterious ◆ friendly.

Careful choice of details and vocabulary allows you to create surprises in your writing. Read the following description:

Skellig

He belched again. His breath stank. Not just the Chinese food, but the stench of the other dead things he ate: the bluebottles, the spiders. He made a gag noise in his throat and he leaned away from the wall like he was going to be sick. I put my hand beneath his shoulder to steady him.
5 I felt something there, something held in by his jacket. He retched. I tried not to breathe, not to smell him. I reached across his back and felt something beneath his other shoulder as well. Like thin arms, folded up. Springy and flexible.

He retched, but he wasn't sick. He leaned back against the wall and
10 I took my hand away.

'Who are you?' I said.

The blackbird sang and sang.

'I wouldn't tell anybody,' I said.

He lifted his hand and looked at it in the torchlight.

15 'I'm nearly nobody,' he said. 'Most of me is Arthur.'

He laughed but he didn't smile.

'Arthur Itis,' he squeaked. 'He's the one that's ruining me bones.'

*from **Skellig** by David Almond*

- What words and phrases in the description make the man seem horrible?
- What details prevent him from seeming like a monster to us?

The English language is rich in **synonyms**. These are words which have a similar meaning. The best way to explore synonyms is to look in a **thesaurus**. A thesaurus will provide you with alternative words. For example if you were to look up the word 'thin' you would find some similar words such as:

bony, emaciated, lean, light, scraggy, skeletal, slender, slight, slim, spare

Use a dictionary to check the differences between the words above.

Which of the words would be best to describe:

- a scary character in a horror story
- an attractive 'hero'?

Activity 11

Look again at the passage from *Skellig* on page 84. Some of the words from the passage have been put in the Word column in the table below. Next to each word is an alternative word the author might have chosen. Choose three of the words under the word heading in the table. Explain why the author chose these words instead of the more obvious alternatives given alongside.

Word	Alternative
scuttled (line 1)	moved
tiptoed (line 3)	walked
snapped (line 7)	broke
scattering (line 9)	ran
peered (line 10)	looked

Drafting

As well as choosing interesting words, it is also a good idea to find different ways of forming sentences. It helps to have sentences of different lengths and which begin in different ways.

Here is the beginning of a short story by John Gordon:

Left in the Dark

The village seemed to be stitched into the hills. A cluster of houses was held by the thread of the stream, and the stream itself was caught under a bridge and hooked around a stone barn in a fold of the heather and bracken. In the October sunshine the hills looked as soft as a quilt.

*from **Left in the Dark** by John Gordon*

Activity 12

Choose three words or phrases from the passage which seem to you to be out of the ordinary. In each case, suggest what an 'ordinary' expression might have been.

Read the following very 'ordinary' passage.

The sky was dark. The sun was hidden behind huge grey clouds. The breeze became stronger. The clouds raced through the sky.
It began to rain.

There's nothing much wrong with that: the sentences are certainly accurate and it paints quite a clear picture. But most of the sentences follow the same pattern: The sky ... , The sun ... , The breeze ... . You can rewrite it in various ways to make it more interesting. Here is one possible redraft:

In the darkening sky, the sun was hidden behind huge grey clouds. As the breeze became stronger, the clouds raced through the sky. It began to rain.

This carries the same meaning but there is more variety: long and short sentences; sentences beginning in different ways.

Activity 13 ICT

Redraft the following extract. Aim to have more variety in the sentences.

The teacher looked around the room. The noise gradually died down. The group in the back corner didn't seem to notice. The teacher slowly walked towards them. The rest of the class followed her with their eyes. She stared down at the chatting group.

10 Different voices

This unit will help you to:

- become more aware of the different ways people speak
- write better dialogue
- write better drama scripts.

Different voices

A dialogue is a conversation between two or more people. Read the following dialogue from the opening of a novel:

It is 1939 and city children are being moved out to the country away from the dangers of bombs. It was the job of volunteers called Billeting Officers to place the children in homes. In this case a middle-aged female Billeting Officer has called round to see a man called Thomas Oakley. Thomas Oakley speaks first:

Goodnight Mr Tom

'Yes. What d'you want?'
'I'm the Billeting Officer for this area.'
'Oh yes, and what's that got to do wi' me?'
5 'Well, Mr, Mr …'
'Oakley. Thomas Oakley.'
'Ah, thank you, Mr Oakley. Mr Oakley, with the declaration of war imminent …'
'I knows all that. Git to the point. What d'you want?' (He noticed a small boy at her side.)
10 'It's him I've come about, I'm on my way to your village hall with the others.'
'What others?'

from ***Goodnight Mr Tom by Michelle Magorian***

Activity 1 ICT

1 Tom and the middle-aged Billeting Officer are clearly different kinds of people.

Find examples of Tom:

- **a** shortening words
- **b** speaking with an accent.

2 Compare how Tom speaks with some of the expressions of the Billeting Officer.

- **a** In what ways is the language of her speech different from Tom's?
- **b** From the way they talk, how would you sum up the differences between the two characters?

In the novel there is more than just the dialogue. The author gives us description as well. Here is the full version of the extract on the previous page:

Goodnight Mr Tom

'Yes,' said Tom bluntly, on opening the front door. 'What d'you want?'

A harassed middle-aged woman in a green coat and felt hat stood on his step. He glanced at the armband on her sleeve. She gave him an awkward smile.

5 'I'm the Billeting Officer for this area,' she began.

'Oh yes, and what's that got to do wi' me?'

She flushed slightly. 'Well, Mr, Mr ....'

'Oakley. Thomas Oakley.'

'Ah, thank you, Mr Oakley.' She paused and took a deep breath. 'Mr

10 Oakley, with the declaration of war imminent ...'

Tom waved his hand. 'I knows all that. Git to the point. What d'you want?' He noticed a small boy at her side.

'It's him I've come about,' she said. 'I'm on my way to your village hall with the others.'

15 'What others?'

She stepped to one side.

*from **Goodnight Mr Tom** by Michelle Magorian*

The author's description of how things are said and what is happening when they are being said, tells you that this is **prose** rather than **drama**.

When you are writing stories and you want to include some dialogue, it is important to add some description. This helps to make the dialogue clearer and easier to follow.

Activity 2

How do the descriptive words in the table below help the reader to hear more clearly how the two characters speak?

Tom	The Billeting Officer
'Yes,' said Tom bluntly.	She paused and took a deep breath.
Tom waved his hand.	She flushed slightly.

Activity 3

a How is the writing in the extract from *Goodnight Mr Tom* set out to help you follow who is talking?

b You might think that it would be simple just to write 'said Mr Oakley' or 'said the Billeting Officer' after each thing they say. Why doesn't the writer do this?

When you are writing your own dialogue, you should try to avoid using 'he said/she said' all the time.

Activity 4 WS

Look at the following sentences. Rewrite them, changing the word 'said' in each case:

a 'Fire!' he said.
b 'Stop tickling me!' he said.
c 'I hate you!' she said.
d 'If you hate the referee clap your hands,' they said.
e 'Oh no, not again!' she said.

If you want to use 'said', it can be a good idea to add some descriptive detail.

For example, instead of simply writing:
'I'd love a puppy,' she said

you could add something:
'I'd love a puppy,' she said, gazing longingly in the pet shop window.

That little piece of description helps you understand how the girl spoke.

Activity 5

Add a short piece of description to each of the following sentences:

a 'I'm warning you, don't push me too far,' he said, ...
b 'Do I have to tidy my bedroom, Mum?' she said, ...
c 'It's lovely to see you,' she said, ...

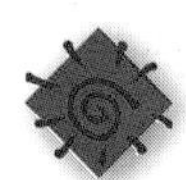

Activity 6

Write a simple conversation between two students who are walking to school. It is their first day. Make one of them quite shy, saying very little, while the other is very outgoing and has a lot to say. Write no more than twenty lines. Concentrate on:

- making it clear who is talking
- avoiding overusing the word 'said'
- adding descriptive detail in between the actual spoken words.

You could begin like this:

'I'm really looking forward to this, Kev. Do you think we'll have homework tonight?'
'Dunno.'
Karenjit looked sharply at Kevin. 'Are you OK?'
'Sort of.'

Before you write out the conversation, think about the situation and the characters. You may like to make a few notes, for example about the two characters.

Once you've written it out, read it through to yourself. Could it be improved? Ask yourself the following questions:

- Do my two characters speak in different ways?
- Does it sound like a real conversation?
- Have I avoided overusing 'said'?
- Have I given enough information about how things are said?

Giving characters an interesting way of speaking helps bring writing to life. In *Harry Potter and the Philosopher's Stone*, Harry has been brought up by his horrible Aunt Petunia and Uncle Vernon, the Dursleys. Their son, Dudley, is given everything he wants, whilst Harry often goes without. The Dursleys have taken Harry into hiding with them but, one day, a stranger appears:

Harry Potter and the Philosopher's Stone

'Boom.' They knocked again. Dudley jerked awake.

'Where's the cannon?' he said stupidly.

There was a crash behind them and Uncle Vernon came skidding into the room. He was holding a rifle in his hands – now they knew what had been in
5 the long, thin package he had brought with them.

'Who's there?' he shouted. 'I warn you – I'm armed!'

There was a pause. Then –

SMASH!

The door was hit with such force that it swung clean off its hinges and
10 with a deafening crash landed flat on the floor.

A giant of a man was standing in the doorway. His face was almost completely hidden by a long, shaggy mane of hair and a wild, tangled beard, but you could make out his eyes, glinting like black beetles under all the hair.

The giant squeezed his way into the hut, stooping so that his head just brushed
15 the ceiling. He bent down, picked up the door and fitted it easily back into its frame. The noise of the storm outside dropped a little. He turned to look at them all.

'Couldn't make us a cup o' tea, could yeh? It's not been an easy journey ...'

He strode over to the sofa where Dudley sat frozen with fear.

'Budge up, yeh great lump,' said the stranger.

20 Dudley squeaked and ran to hide behind his mother, who was crouching, terrified, behind Uncle Vernon.

'An' here's Harry!' said the giant.

Harry looked up into the fierce, wild shadowy face and saw that the beetle eyes were crinkled in a smile.

25 'Las' time I saw you, you was only a baby,' said the giant. 'Yeh look a lot like yer dad, but yeh've got yer mum's eyes.'

Uncle Vernon made a funny rasping noise.

'I demand that you leave at once, sir!' he said. 'You are breaking and entering!'

'Ah, shut up, Dursley, yeh great prune,' said the giant; he reached over the back
30 of the sofa, jerked the gun out of Uncle Vernon's hands, bent it into a knot as easily as if it had been made of rubber, and threw it into a corner of the room.

Uncle Vernon made another funny noise, like a mouse being trodden on.

'Anyway – Harry,' said the giant, turning his back on the Dursleys, 'a very happy birthday to yeh. Got summat fer yeh here – I mighta sat on it at some point, but it'll
35 taste all right.'

From an inside pocket of his black overcoat he pulled a slightly squashed box. Harry opened it with trembling fingers. Inside was a large, sticky chocolate cake with *Happy Birthday Harry* written on it in green icing.

Harry looked up at the giant. He meant to say thank you, but the words got lost
40 on the way to his mouth, and what he said instead was, 'Who are you?'

The giant chuckled.

'True, I haven't introduced meself. Rubeus Hagrid, Keeper of Keys and Grounds at Hogwarts.'

from ***Harry Potter and the Philosopher's Stone*** *by J.K. Rowling*

Activity 7

1 The author has arranged this scene so that Hagrid clearly does most of the talking. Look at what he says and how he says it.

Choose some examples of his language that might suggest he is a bit 'rough-and-ready'.

2 Uncle Vernon talks in a different way from Hagrid.

a How would you describe his language?

b What does his way of talking tell you about him?

Trying to capture different voices is a good way of bringing interest into your writing. There are different ways of doing this. Here are a few of them:

- You can try to spell words as they sound when spoken by some people. For example; 'I would have ...' can be shortened to 'I would've ...' or even to the incorrect but commonly spoken 'I would of ...'
- Many people speak in non-standard English. You can use this fact to help you in your writing. It can help to show differences between characters. For example, 'I don't know' can be written as 'Dunno'. What kinds of characters are likely to say this?
- You can introduce slang when appropriate. When you are trying to capture the different ways young and old people speak, use of slang is an obvious feature. Can you think of words and phrases you and your friends use that are unlikely to be used by older people?
- Characters can be given mannerisms. Some people, for example, keep saying 'You know' when they talk. Others use 'Erm' a lot.
- You may live in an area with a strong dialect which you might be able to capture. The writer Ian McMillan, who is from South Yorkshire, tells the following story:

> I was in the barber's the other day; the room was full of South Yorkshiremen, so there was complete silence. A man stuck his head round the door. AR? he said. NO said the barber. REYT said the man. Loosely translated, that would read 'Hello, barber, I wonder if you could fit me in before half past five?' 'No sir, as you can see I've got a shop full.' 'Oh, all right then, I'll call back later.'

- Think of people you know well (don't forget yourself!). What speaking habits do they have? Think about your friends and family, but also about groups of people like teachers. Do they speak in the same way as you, or do they have their own way of speaking?

Activity 8 WS

Choose one of the following situations and write out the dialogue. Try to capture two different voices which show two different ways of speaking.

1 A teacher is talking to an 'awkward' student.
You could begin:

'Where is your homework? It was due in this morning.'
'Dunno, miss.'

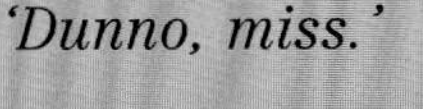

2 A new student arrives at a school. S/he comes from a different area.
A student is asked to 'look after' him/her.
You could begin:

'How ya doin'?'
'I beg your pardon?'

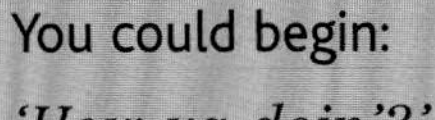

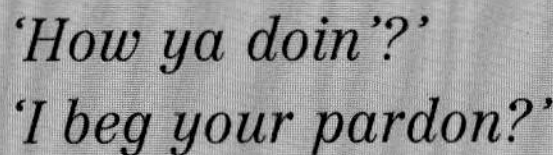

3 There's a knock at the door. You open it. Write the dialogue that follows.
You could begin:

'Yeah?'
'I'm terribly sorry to disturb you.'

Writing a play script

Even though there may be lots of speaking in stories, we most often read them inside our heads, silently. Plays are written to be acted and, therefore, read aloud, so it's especially important to try to capture how different people speak.

In the following scene, Kevin and Bee are at school. Bee used to be best friends with a girl called Julie, but recently she has joined in with Kevin and his mates when they have teased and bullied Julie. Bee has been feeling a bit guilty about the way she has been treating Julie.

	Kevin	Bee! Have you heard!
	Bee	What?
	Kevin	You haven't heard!
	Bee	Haven't heard what?
5	**Kevin**	About Julie Mills.
	Bee	Yes. Course I have.
	Kevin	Oh. Right.
	Bee	Kev! Wait!
	Kevin	What?
10	**Bee**	Go on. Tell me.
	Kevin	I thought you knew.
	Bee	Tell me!
	Kevin	About Julie's accident?
	Mr Murphy	Come on, Kevin Proctor. Your form's in assembly already.
15	**Kevin**	Sorry, sir.
	Bee	Wait! Kevin! Wait!
	Mr Murphy	And you too, young lady. Have you registered yet?
	Bee	Please, Mr Murphy! Can I just ask ... Kevin! Wait!
	Kevin	He'll do us!
20	**Bee**	What happened to Julie?
	Kevin	She got knocked down.
	Mr Murphy	I'm counting, Proctor.
	Kevin	Outside her school. She was running away ...
	Mr Murphy	Three ...
25	**Bee**	I don't believe you, Kevin.
	Mr Murphy	Two ...
	Kevin	Cross me heart and hope to die.
	Bee	When? How?
	Kevin	She was taken to ...
30	**Mr Murphy**	NOW!
	Kevin	Sorry, sir. Hospital.

*from **How Green You Are!** by Berlie Doherty*

Activity 9 WS ICT

1 There is really only one piece of information in this long conversation – that Julie has been knocked down in an accident – but think about the way the writer lets this information emerge:

  a Why does Bee say 'Course I have' when she doesn't know what he's talking about?

  b Why does the writer introduce the teacher halfway through the scene? How does it delay the information?

  c In what ways is this dialogue like real-life conversation?

2 There are some things you have to work out for yourself if you want to perform this scene. The writer doesn't give you any stage directions about how to say the lines.

  Think carefully about:

  a how you think the speaker is feeling as they say each line and how they speak it

  b what they might be doing as they speak.

  Copy out the scene. After each line put a stage direction in brackets which will help actors speak the lines. You might begin like this:

Kevin Bee! Have you heard! *(He's excited – the news is dramatic)*
Bee What? *(Calmly – she's unaware)*
Kevin You haven't heard! *(He can't believe she doesn't know)*
Bee Haven't heard what? *(A little impatient)*

In the following scene Jim is being placed with foster parents by his social worker, Tony. The foster parents are Mr and Mrs Welland. They have a daughter, Miranda, who is the same age as Jim. This is Jim's first visit to the Wellands' home. He is clutching his most treasured possession, a rolled-up poster of Mount Everest. Read the scene aloud. You will need five speakers.

	Mrs Welland	Hello, Jim.
		Jim ignores her. Tony looks disapproving.
	Tony	Jim.
		Jim responds in a lifeless way.
5	**Jim**	Hello.
		Mr Welland goes to take the poster.
	Mr Welland	Shall I take that?
		Jim defends the poster.
	Mrs Welland	You're just in time for lunch. You too, Tony.
10	**Jim**	I don't like it here.
	Tony	Give it a chance will you?
		He turns to Mrs Welland.
		Thanks.
		Tony sits down. Jim follows suit as do Miranda
15		*and Mr Welland. Jim puts his poster by the table.*
	Mr Welland	Introduce yourself, Miranda.
	Miranda	Hello, Jim.
		Jim grunts something.
	Tony	I think this is going to take everyone a bit of time.
20	**Mrs Welland**	Of course.
		Mrs Welland puts a large bowl of food in the
		middle of the table.
		I bet you're starving, Jim.
		Jim looks suspiciously at the bowl.
25	**Jim**	No.
	Mrs Welland	Well, I hope you don't mind us eating.
		She starts serving up.
	Mr Welland	It's couscous. Sort of an African meal. It's
		made from … what's it made from?
30	**Mrs Welland**	Semolina. Have you had it before, Jim?
	Jim	No.
	Mrs Welland	Oh.
	Jim	But my hamster did.
	Mrs Welland	Oh?
35	**Jim**	Then it died.
	Mr Welland	We weren't sure what you'd like to eat. We're
		vegetarian.
		Jim looks appalled.

	Jim	What?
40	**Miranda**	We don't eat meat.
	Tony	I did tell you.
	Jim	No beefburgers, no sausages, no bacon?
	Mr Welland	Of course, you'll be able to eat whatever you want. *Jim stands up.*
	Jim	Beam me up, Scotty.
45	**Tony**	Jim, we've talked about this. You're not going to feel settled straightaway. It's just as strange for the Wellands, remember. You've got to get used to each other.
	Jim	I don't want to get used. I don't want to be here.

from ***Burning Everest*** *by Adrian Flynn*

Activity 10

1 Answer the following questions. Support your answers with evidence from the text:

a How do the Wellands try to make Jim feel welcome?

b How does Jim respond to them?

c Why do you think the speeches are quite short?

d How does Jim speak differently from the adults?

2 Look again at the lines about the couscous, beginning 'It's couscous ...' and ending 'Beam me up, Scotty.' The writer could have written it differently. It could have been written like this:

Mr Welland	It's couscous. Sort of an African meal. It's made from semolina.
Mrs Welland	Have you had it before, Jim?
Jim	No. But my hamster did. Then it died.

What are the differences between this and the original version? What effect do they have?

Activity 11

1 Can you explain why the writer wrote this part of the scene as he did? Give reasons for your answer.

2 How do you think the audience respond to Jim's remark about the hamster? How does it change the atmosphere?

Later in the scene the adults leave the room and Miranda and Jim are left on their own. Jim has his back to Miranda and is staring out of the window.

Miranda There's a football team at school, if you're any good at football.
No response from Jim.
Most of the teachers are mad, but the kids are all right. They're a good laugh, some of them. What was your old school like? 5
Still no response.
I bet you're missing your mum. I don't blame you. I'd miss mine.
Still no response. Miranda gets up and takes the horror eyes out of a pocket [Miranda got the joke horror eyes out of a breakfast cereal packet earlier in the day]. 10
I wish you wouldn't talk so much. You're making the eyes pop out of my head.
She puts the eyes on and walks towards Jim. She mimics him.
I hate it already. I'm not going to like it. I'm never going to like it. 15
Jim responds angrily.

Jim Are you taking the mickey?
Jim turns around and is taken aback by Miranda's appearance. He half laughs in spite of himself. Miranda answers defiantly. 20

Miranda Yes, I am.
She takes off the horror eyes and goes back to the table.
What's your poster of?
Jim goes over to it.

25 **Jim** Leave it alone.

Miranda All right. I only wanted to look. What is it?

Jim Chomolungma.

Miranda What?
Jim unrolls it.

30 **Jim** Mount Everest, stupid. It's really called Chomolungma.

Activity 12

This part of the scene is very different from what went before. The situation has developed. Look at it again and answer the following questions:

a Why is Miranda more successful than the adults at getting somewhere with Jim?

b Why do you think the writer gives Miranda such a long speech?

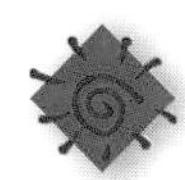

Activity 13

'Awkward' situations can lead to good drama. Choose one of the following situations as the basis of a scene you can write:

a A group of four friends are playing. A new boy/girl has moved into the street and is introducing him/herself.

b A young person has been accused of shoplifting. The shop manager has called the police. The police officer, manager and young person are in the manager's office. The young person's mum or dad has been telephoned and is just about to appear.

c The parents of two children have been divorced for about a year. Mum or Dad has met a new boy/girlfriend and brings him/her home for the first time so that s/he can meet the children.

Before you write your scene you could try improvising it in a small group. But remember that the focus should be on words rather than action.

As you write your scene think about the following:

- showing differences between characters by the way they speak
- the importance of stage directions
- making changes in the atmosphere.

If you have access to a computer, it will help you write out your scene. Drama scripts are set out in ways that make them easy to follow. You could use **bold** for the characters' names and *italics* for stage directions. It makes them easier to read. If you don't have access to a computer, you need to think of easy ways of showing which character is talking and where there are stage directions.

11 Playing with words

This unit will help you to:
- sequence ideas in imaginative ways
- use rhyme in poetry
- understand and use similes.

Word Association

Word Association is a game in which someone says a word and the next person has to say a word that is in some way connected with the first word. The next person then has to say a word which has something to do with the second word and so on. For example, you might get a sequence of words like:

TREE > WOOD > OAK > ACORN > SQUIRREL > TAIL > DOG > COLLAR
You can use this idea to write poems.

You begin by writing down a word. Then you write down a word that is connected with it, then a word connected with that word and so on. Here's an example beginning with the word 'sky':

sky → clouds → rain → umbrella

That could lead to a poem of four lines based on those key words. In the first line you would use the word 'sky', in the second line 'cloud', and so on, for example:

Beautiful deep blue **sky**,
Till slate **clouds** bring
Grey sheets of **rain**. Dismal till
Bright multi-coloured **umbrellas** float above the pavements.

Activity 1 WS ICT

Write your own four-line poem.
Begin by associating four words. The first one is 'Africa'.

There is another way of writing poems based upon word association. Each word must be connected in some way with the word before it. To make it interesting, there are some other rules:

- There must be eight lines.
- There must be four words in each line.
- The lines have to rhyme in pairs.

Here is an example:

clock hands fingers nails
hammer blow wind gales

storm rain water sea
fish chips potato pea

green grass cow Jersey
island country river Mersey

Liverpool city bank money
wages work bees honey

Activity 2

Now try your own version of an eight-line poem. You can begin with any word you choose. There is no correct answer for this exercise. The important thing is to try and have fun.

Rhyming can be fun. You will be very familiar with it. Where do you find rhyming outside poetry books? How many different uses of rhyme can you think of?

A pair of rhymes is called a **couplet**. Choose one of the pairs of rhymes in the box below and see if you can write a couplet. For example, if the pair of words you chose was *bee* and *tea* you might end up with a couplet like:

I hope you don't think I'm stealing, bee,
When I take your honey for my tea.

◆ frog/dog ◆ fears/ears ◆ teacher/creature ◆ furry/worry ◆ refrigerator/alligator

It's possible to make quite ordinary things seem special by using rhyme. Here is a poem about the sort of things you can find in a market:

Jamaica Market

Honey, pepper, leaf-green limes,
Pagan fruit whose names are rhymes,
Mangoes, breadfruit, ginger-roots,
Granadillas, bamboo-shoots,
5 Cho-cho, ackees, tangerines,
Lemons, purple Congo-beans,
Sugar, okras, kola-nuts,
Citrons, hairy coconuts,
Fish, tobacco, native hats,
10 Gold bananas, woven mats,
Plantains, wild thyme, pallid leeks
Pigeons with their scarlet beaks,
Oranges and saffron yams,
Baskets, ruby guava jams,
15 Turtles, goat-skins, cinnamon,
Allspice, conch-shells, golden rum.
Black skins, babel – and the sun
That burns all colours into one.

Agnes Maxwell-Hall

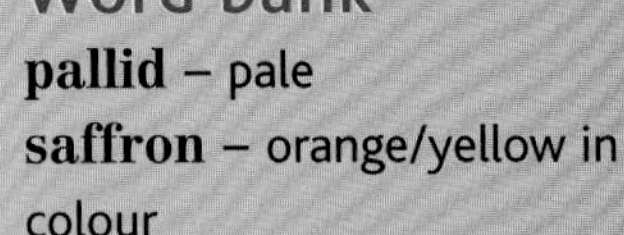

Word bank

pallid – pale
saffron – orange/yellow in colour
babel – a scene of noise and confusion

Activity 3 ◆ICT

Try to write your own poem based on a list of nouns like this. You could try writing about a local market, or a supermarket, or the street, the city or anywhere you like.

But, before you start letting your imagination run riot, be practical: it's a good idea to draft poems. Drafting doesn't have to mean writing and re-writing. The first draft of your poem may be a simple list of the words you would like to use. The second stage might be to group the words as they rhyme and to think of other rhyming words.

Rhyme is a kind of pattern and is one of the things that makes poetry obviously different from prose. It is often used in poems with a strong **rhythm**. The following poem rhymes and it also has a very strong rhythm. Practise reading the poem aloud.

The Sound Collector

A stranger called this morning
Dressed all in black and grey
Put every sound into a bag
And carried them away.

5 The whistling of the kettle
The turning of the lock
The purring of the kitten
The ticking of the clock

10 The popping of the toaster
The crunching of the flakes
When you spread the marmalade
The scraping noise it makes

The hissing of the frying-pan
15 The ticking of the grill
The bubbling of the bathtub
As it starts to fill

The drumming of the raindrops
On the window-pane
20 When you do the washing-up
The gurgle of the drain

The crying of the baby
The squeaking of the chair
The swishing of the curtain
The creaking of the stair

25 A stranger called this morning
He didn't leave his name
Left us only silence
Life will never be the same.

Roger McGough

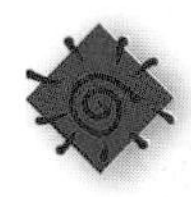

Activity 4 ICT

Using the same pattern as Roger McGough, try to write your own poem about sounds.

When you rhyme you are connecting different words, connecting them because they sound similar. Sometimes rhyming words have obvious connections, like *star* and *far*, *frown* and *down*. Sometimes they seem to be opposites, like *sad* and *glad*, *light* and *night*. Often they seem to have no connection at all but poets often bring ideas together in quite entertaining ways:

Alligator

From Sydney Zoo
An Alligator
Was put on board
A flying freighter.
5 He ate the pilot
And the navigator
Then asked for more
With mashed potater.

Spike Milligan

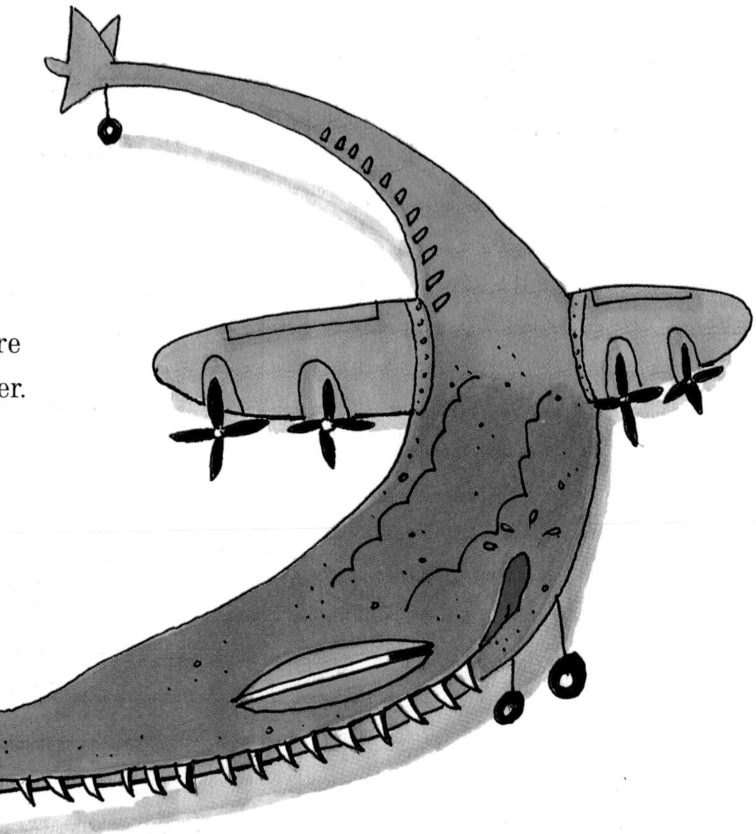

Spike Milligan uses four rhyming words as the basis for his poem. He's 'cheated' a little with one. Which one?

Activity 5

Try writing your own poems based on four rhymes like the one above. For practice, you could try to make a poem out of one of the following sets of four rhymes:

footballer / taller / smaller / brawler
lorry / worry / quarry / sorry

But try to come up with your own four rhyming words.

Making comparisons

Poets make connections in other ways. Very often they describe things by comparing them with something else. Look at the following comparisons and see if you can work out what is being described. Match each poem to the correct picture.

1 A drifting, fringed, lampshade
in the dusk
of the deep.

Stewart Henderson

2 ... sudden fiery flowers
That burst upon the night.

James Reeves

3 Grazing down on the carpet
pasture:
Cow with electric bones.

Kit Wright

4 Chinese characters
in the lower sky

Douglas Dunn

5 he duels with himself and woos
his women customers

Craig Raine

6 who carries his pregnant belly
in the hammock of his leotard

like a melon wedged in a
shopping-bag...

Christopher Reid

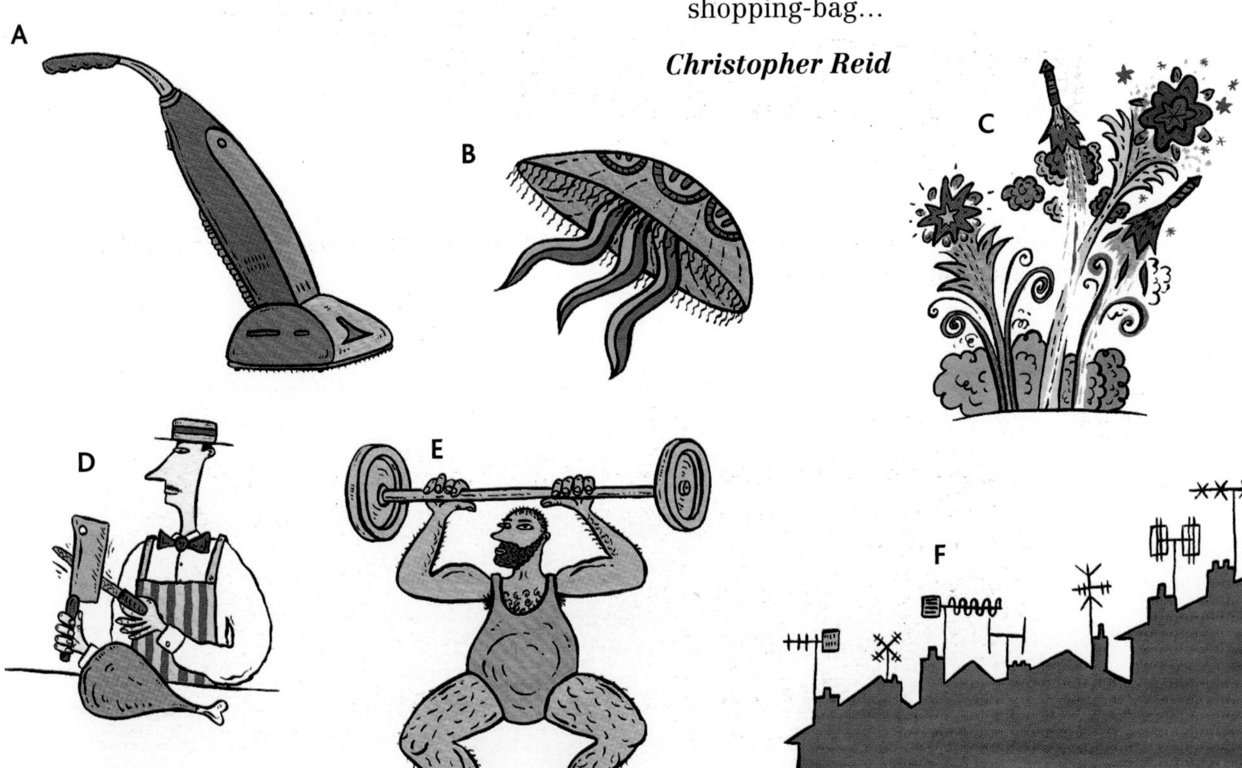

Similes

When poets compare two things using the words 'like' or 'as', they are using what is called a **simile**.

The following stanzas are from a long poem written in the nineteenth century. The skipper of a sailing ship called the *Hesperus* has taken his daughter on a voyage, but the ship sails into trouble. This is the section that decribes the fate of the ship:

The Wreck of the *Hesperus*

And fast through the midnight dark and drear,
 Through the whistling sleet and snow,
Like a sheeted ghost, the vessel swept
 Towards the reef of Norman's Woe.

5 And ever the fitful gusts between
 A sound came from the land;
It was the sound of the trampling surf,
 On the rocks and the hard sea-sand.

The breakers were right beneath her bows.
10 She drifted a dreary wreck,
And a whooping billow swept the crew
 Like icicles from her deck.

She struck where the white and fleecy waves
 Looked soft as carded wool,
15 But the cruel rocks, they gored her side
 Like the horns of an angry bull.

Her rattling shrouds, all sheathed in ice,
 With the masts went by the board;
Like a vessel of glass, she stove and sank,
20 Ho! Ho! The breakers roared!

*from **The Wreck of the Hesperus** by Henry Wadsworth Longfellow*

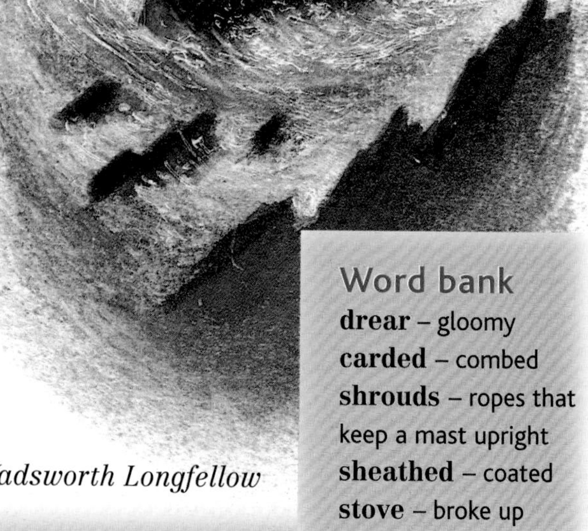

Word bank

drear – gloomy
carded – combed
shrouds – ropes that keep a mast upright
sheathed – coated
stove – broke up

Activity 6 WS ICT

1 a How many similes can you find in these stanzas? Write them down.

 b Choose three of them and write an explanation of them. For example, why are the rocks compared to an angry bull? What picture is the writer painting for you?

2 Try writing descriptions of the following, using similes. Your descriptions should include the word 'like'.

◆ a car ◆ a school bell ◆ a wasp ◆ an electric kettle ◆ a baby ◆ night ◆ clouds.

You can write longer poems based on similes. Here's a poem about something which the writer compares with lots of other things:

Like the white curls from a gigantic beard
Drifting across the barber's shop floor
In the breeze from the open door;
Like the broken parts of the ice floe
5 Afloat on the blue of the ocean,
Drifting southward from the Pole;
Like a heavily laden treasure fleet
In a light wind on a calm sea,
Hardly moving with all sails set;
10 Like suds of foam from a waterfall
That lathers the rocks at its foot,
Gliding over a tranquil pool;
Like wool from a fleece,
Like smoke from a fire,
15 Like islands in the sky.

Stanley Cook

If you hadn't worked it out before, the last line should help you to see what is being described – clouds.

Activity 7 WS ICT

Write your own simile poem. You'll need to spend some time thinking about what to describe and then what you could compare it with. It would be a good idea to make a spider diagram to help you draft your ideas. For example, if you wanted to describe a football crowd you might draft out something like this:

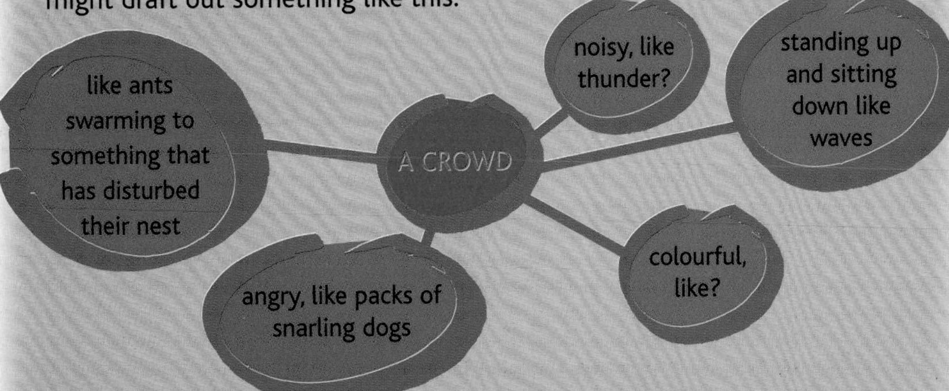

Once you've planned a few ideas, think about which ideas are best and the best order for them. You could call your poem *Simile Poem* or, if you want to help the reader guess, give it the name of whatever it is you are describing.

Assignment 3

Your teacher will advise you as to which of these tasks you are to complete.

1 **PROSE**
Imagine you are a traveller. You are on your own. You find yourself in one of the following settings:

- stranded on a distant planet
- stranded on a small island
- visiting a new city
- lost in a forest
- in the place you live now but one hundred years in the future.

Write a description of the setting.

You will need to use your imagination to create the setting. Think of what you might be able to see, hear, smell and touch.

2 **POETRY**
Produce a poetry album. A photograph album is a book in which you keep important photographs. Your poetry album should contain a series of poems about people who are important in your life.

So, for example, there might be a couple of little poems about your sister – one about her good side and one about the bad! Then there might be a poem about a favourite aunt, and so forth.

It's up to you to decide what shape and style you want your poems to be in.

3 **DRAMA and DIALOGUE**
Adults and children often disagree or argue about a variety of things – untidy bedrooms, staying out, friends, behaviour and so forth.

Write a scene in which an adult (or adults) is arguing with a child (or children). Write it either as a play script or as a piece of dialogue in story form.

4 **PROSE / POETRY / DRAMA**
The purpose of this assignment is to use all three kinds of writing to create a picture of a place. Choose an area you know very well: it might be the street you live on, or the town centre, or a holiday place you know.
Then:

a **Write a script of conversation** that might take place in this area. It might be two people talking about the bus service, or two children talking about what they are planning to do that day, or two people talking about a local feature (complaining about noisy teenagers perhaps!). Your conversation could give an idea about what kind of place it is – friendly? violent? quiet?

b **Write a poem** about one important feature of the place. It might be a building, or a person, or a street. You will need to decide what kind of poem you write.

c **Write a description, in prose,** of the place. You might choose to focus on some particular part rather than describe the whole place.

The title of the three pieces will be the name of the place.

B2 Writing non-fiction

In the last unit you learned how to write prose, poems and play scripts. All of these were written using your imagination; you had made them up. They did not necessarily deal with events that had really taken place.

What are non-fiction texts?

In this unit you will learn how to write non-fiction texts. These are texts which deal with facts, opinions and events. They are written for many different reasons:

- to give information
- to give instructions
- to explain
- to set down the true facts of someone's life
- to give advice
- to persuade
- to put forward a point of view.

Non-fiction texts are written in a variety of styles. They can look very different on the page.

Learning to write non-fiction texts

In this unit you will find out how different types of non-fiction are written before you write your own examples. You will learn how to write:

- letters
- invitations
- reports
- advertisements
- instructions and explanations
- posters.

You will need to use the following skills:

- planning
- making notes before you write
- using capital letters and full stops in the right place
- using commas, question marks and exclamation marks correctly
- using paragraphs
- explaining your ideas clearly and sensibly
- using the right sort of language to appeal to a particular type of reader
- setting out your work properly according to the type of text you are writing
- re-drafting your work.

13 Audience and purpose

This unit will help you to:
- choose the right words to suit your readers
- use suitable pictures to appeal to your readers
- use different ways of presenting your work according to its purpose.

Audience

Every piece of writing is written with a certain type of person or a particular person in mind. For example, you might send a postcard to a friend from your holidays or write a thank-you letter to a relative who has sent you a present. These are people whom you know personally. You have a particular person in mind when you start to write.

Dear Simon,
It's horrible here! It hasn't stopped raining and there is nothing to do. I'm so glad I was allowed to bring my Nintendo. I play it all day. I've got really good at that driving game of yours but I'm bored with it now. My Mum won't give me any money to buy a new game. We might as well have stayed at home. See you next week. Matt

Dear Nanny,

Thank you very much for my CD. It's the best! I have played it over and over again. Dad says he knows all the words now which is really funny.

I had a really, really good birthday. I went swimming with some of my friends from school, then we came back home and ate pizzas. I had the biggest chocolate cake ever, everyone had two slices and there was still some left! I've been having it in my packed lunch all week. Better than sandwiches any day!

School is OK. I am starting to learn French which is difficult. Mum says that if I keep practising it I can go to France on an exchange in Year 10.

Thanks again for my birthday present. When you come to visit again, I'll play it to you.

See you soon., Lots and Lots of love. Vicky
XXXX

Some pieces of writing are written for larger groups of people who are not known to the writer. For example, the page listing TV programmes in a newspaper is written for a very large number of people.

tuesday 17 AUG

BBC1

6.00 Business Breakfast Financial and business news. **78497**
7.00 BBC Breakfast News (T) **24098**
9.00 to 10.50 Children's BBC
9.00 Kenan and Kel (T)(R) 91611 **9.30 Smart** (T)(R) 9032982
9.55 Willy Fog (T)(R) 1886543 **10.20 Teletubbies** (T) 8122369
10.50 The New Adventures of Superman *Double Jeopardy:* Lois persuades Clark to cancel their honeymoon in Hawaii. (T)(R) **5022678**
11.35 Big Strong Girls *Hull:* DIY series. Home Improvement experts Fiona Quigley and Siobhan Palmer travel to Hull to educate Ian Young on the finer points of DIY. **7047366**
12.00 BBC News (T), **Regional News** and **Weather**
12.05 The Rankin Challenge
NEW *Nostalgia:* A new series of the cookery challenge. Chef Paul Rankin visits Coleraine, in Northern Ireland. **8525727**
12.35 Lion Country Life at the stately home of Longleat, its village and safari park. The iguanas in pets corner are losing their tails. (R) **6605982**
1.00 BBC News (T) and **Weather 27185**
1.30 Regional News (T) and **Weather 51814494**
1.40 Neighbours Hannah meets a rock star and Tad's parents are behaving strangely. (T) **59154814** ***For cast, see page 19***
2.05 Ironside *To Kill a Cop:* Crime drama series. Det Sgt Brown is determined to prove that Frank Vincent killed a policeman. (R) **6452098**
2.55 Can't Cook, Won't Cook With Ainsley Harriott. (T) **6701920**
3.25 to 5.35 Children's BBC
3.25 Little Bear *Mitzi's Little Monster/Simon Says/Applesauce:* Triple-bill of animation. 8459036 **3.45 Arthur** *Arthur vs the Very Mean Crossing Guard/DW's Very Bad Mood:* Double-bill of animated adventures. 308982

The person or people the writing is intended for is known as the **audience**.

All writers have to think carefully about the audience before they begin to write so that they can choose the right words, and sometimes pictures, to appeal to the audience they have in mind.

Who would you have in mind if you were writing the following:
- a party invitation
- a shopping list for Christmas presents
- a telephone message?

When we read a text, there are clues to tell us who the audience is. Pictures can be an important clue. Texts written for young children usually have pictures, which are often brightly coloured, and they do not usually have a lot of words on the page. Sometimes they also keep the writing to small sections at a time.

Talk about this with a partner and see if you can explain why this is. You should be able to find at least three reasons.

Activity 1 ICT

Look carefully at the two texts below. Copy the three headings below into your book and make notes on each of the texts under these headings:

- Which audience?
- A lot of writing or a little?
- Easy words or difficult words? (Find examples of each and write them down.)

Refer to the texts to help you find reasons for your answers.

Part One OUTBREAK OF WAR IN EUROPE

THE START OF THE WAR

On 1 September 1939 German troops poured across Poland's border. Within two days both Britain and France declared war on Germany.

In Britain the Government and people prepared for air raids. Children were evacuated from London; hospital patients were sent home to make room for the expected causalities; and cinemas, theatres and other public places were closed. The civilian population was ordered to carry gas masks at all times.

Activity 2 WS

Design your own party invitation. Before you start, think carefully about the people who will read it. They are your audience. Try to choose your words and pictures to suit them. Plan your ideas following the list below:

- What sort of party is it? A birthday party? A Halloween party? A Christmas party? A party for younger children?
- Where will the party be held? Date? Time?
- Do you want a reply?
- Will you include pictures as well as words?

Make a rough draft first so that you can improve it before you design the final version.

Purpose

Writing is an important part of most people's daily lives. Often we take it for granted and write, or watch others write, without giving it much thought. However, everything we write is written for a reason. This is called the purpose of a piece of writing.

For example, the purpose of a birthday card is to send a greeting, and a poster is written to tell you about a future event such as a concert or pantomime. Some texts are written to explain something, for example, how to look after a pet. Some texts are written to instruct, for example, instructions on how to play a computer game.

Other texts such as telephone messages, or train timetables, are written to inform or give you certain information. Texts can also persuade someone to do something. For example, an advertisement can persuade you to buy a particular item. Sometimes texts such as joke books, stories or poems are written to entertain.

Activity 3 ICT

List six different types of texts and the reasons why they are written. Set out your list like this:

TYPE OF TEXT	PURPOSE

Activity 4 WS

The texts opposite are examples of writing with the purpose to instruct, to explain or to inform. Read them and match each text to its correct purpose. Write your answers in note form in a chart like the one below, and say how you were able to decide what the purpose of each one was. The first one is done for you.

	TYPE OF TEXT	PURPOSE	REASONS
TEXT 1	cookery book	to instruct	Pictures and writing show how to do something
TEXT 2			
TEXT 3			
TEXT 4			

1

Swimming Fish Cakes

Handy Hints:

- ❖ Ask a grown-up to open the can of tuna with a can opener, as this can be dangerous and you might cut yourself.
- ❖ You could make the fish cakes up to several hours in advance, if you like. Keep them in the fridge until you are ready to cook and eat them.

YOU WILL NEED THESE INGREDIENTS

Serves 4

25g (1oz) butter

3 large potatoes

1 egg

dash of milk

200g (7oz) can tuna chunks in brine, drained

75g (3oz) fresh breadcrumbs

pepper

oil, for shallow frying

For the garnish:

4 peas

a few sprigs of fresh curly parsley

1/2 cucumber peeled, cut in half lengthways and very thinly sliced

4 slices of lemon,
4 thin slices of tomato

Special equipment:
vegetable peeler, potato masher, can opener

2

TEETH'S LITTLE 'HEROES'

- **Bread sticks** – plain, cheese flavoured or with sesame seeds
- **Vegetable sticks** – carrots and celery are great to nibble on
- **Homemade plain popcorn**
- **Low fat crisps** – not too often though
- **Nuts like peanuts** – choose the plain ones. Remember, some children may be allergic to peanuts, and don't give nuts to children under 5 in case they choke.
- **Tea cakes or fruit buns** – the ones without icing on top – with a little of your favourite spread if you want
- **Scones or plain muffins** (not the ones which look like little cakes) and a thin layer of a spread that you like
- **Fresh fruit and a carton of yogurt or fromage frais.**

Try to have breakfast, maybe cereal with milk, before you leave for school – it's much better for you and your teeth than having a sweet snack on the way to school, or during the morning.

If you don't have breakfast at home, try these healthy snacks. They're good to have straight after school too:

- **Sandwiches** – try cheese, hard boiled egg, marmite or peanut butter on your favourite type of bread. These can be made the night before if you want, and left in the fridge until it's time to go to school. They're so easy to munch at any time
- **Cheese (hard or soft) and crackers, oatcakes or crispbread**

Drinks

Good to have at any time:

- **A glass of milk**
- **Homemade milkshakes** – use milk and add puréed fresh fruit or canned unsweetened fruit for flavour – no sugar!
- **Water.**

Best to have only with meals:

- **Unsweetened fruit juice** – try fruit juice made up half and half with tap water or fizzy bottled water
- **Sugar-free squash, cordial and fizzy drinks**
- **Ordinary squash, cordial and fizzy drinks.**

3

Bobby Roberts
Super
CIRCUS
TRADITIONAL CIRCUS AT ITS BEST
HEALD GREEN
CHEADLE
GRIFFIN FARM, Wilmslow Road B 5358
Monday 21st SEPT to
Sunday 27th SEPT inclusive
Monday at 7.30pm ONLY
Tuesday to Friday at 5pm & 7.30pm
Saturday at 2.30pm & 5pm Sunday at 2.30pm ONLY
DIAL-A-SEAT 0860 787745 or
0421 888032
Box Office open on site from Monday 21st Sept from 9am daily or Book Now at J & H Metcalf Newsagents, 183 Stockport Road, Cheadle, Tel. 0161 491 2500. Miss Ellies World Travel, 348 Wellington Road, Stockport, Tel. 0161-431 0265
PRICES
Rear Centre Ringside
ADULTS £6 £9 £12
CHILD/O.A.P. £4 £6 £8

4

YOUR DELIVERY

This delivery note is for your information only.

Please check the contents of your parcel against the details shown overleaf. If there is anything incorrect or an item is faulty or damaged, you can return it for a replacement. Please enclose this delivery note with the item and please make sure that you get a receipt from the post office or carrier.

The total amount due will be shown on your next statement. All payments must be sent to us within 10 days of receipt of your statement.

Please make your cheque or postal order payable to your club quoting your membership number on the reverse. You can also pay by credit card by completing the reverse of the order form.

Presentation of information

As you have seen, different types of text are set out differently on the page. The way they are set out is called the presentation.

For example, an invitation has just a few lines of writing and a recipe has the ingredients written in a list so that they can be easily read. Sometimes the writer needs to use **bold type** or CAPITAL LETTERS to make important pieces of information stand out. Pictures and diagrams are also used in some texts. These **devices** are called presentational features.

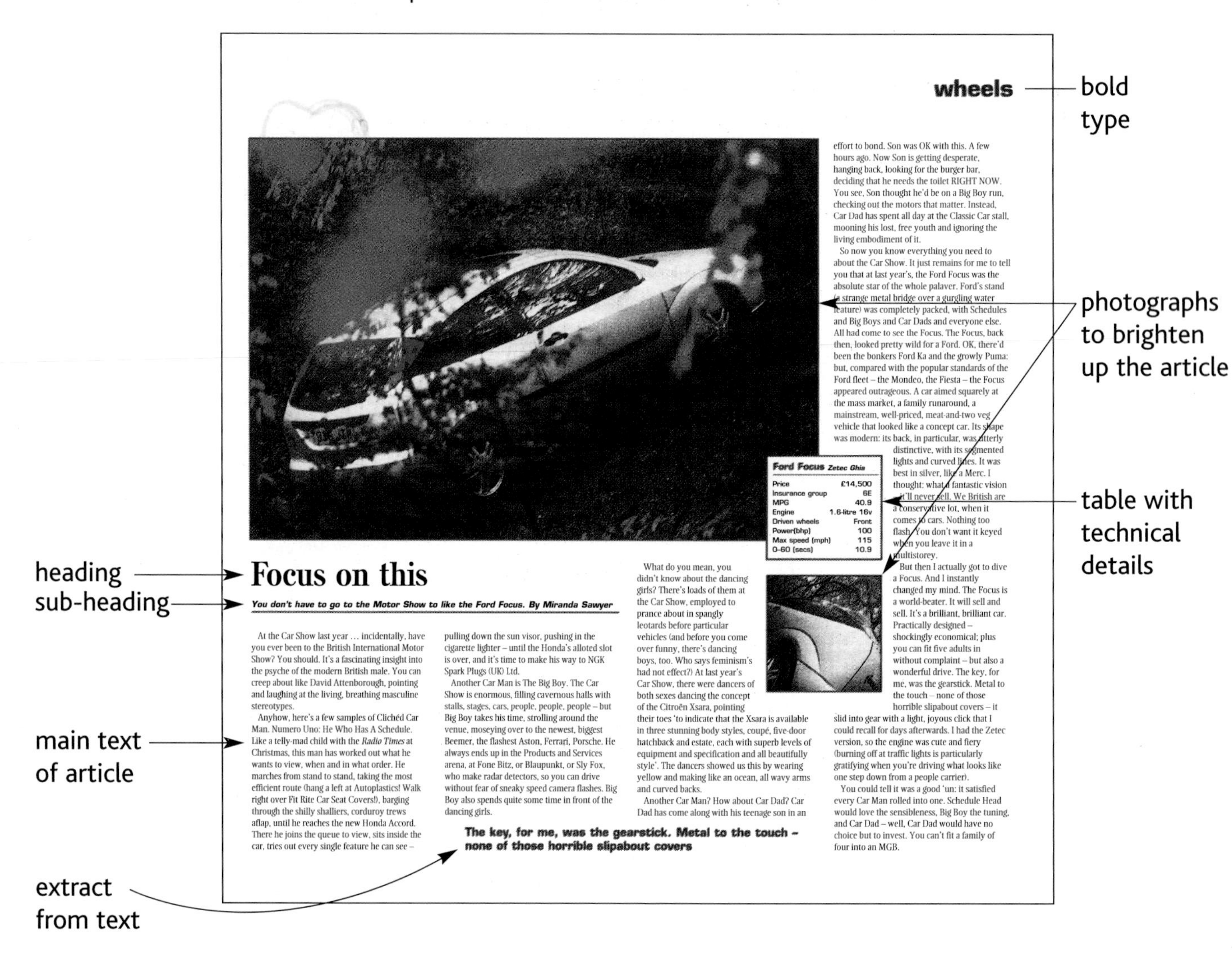

wheels

Focus on this

You don't have to go to the Motor Show to like the Ford Focus. By Miranda Sawyer

At the Car Show last year … incidentally, have you ever been to the British International Motor Show? You should. It's a fascinating insight into the psyche of the modern British male. You can creep about like David Attenborough, pointing and laughing at the living, breathing masculine stereotypes.

Anyhow, here's a few samples of Clichéd Car Man. Numero Uno: He Who Has A Schedule. Like a telly-mad child with the *Radio Times* at Christmas, this man has worked out what he wants to view, when and in what order. He marches from stand to stand, taking the most efficient route (hang a left at Autoplastics! Walk right over Fit Rite Car Seat Covers!), barging through the shilly shalliers, corduroy trews aflap, until he reaches the new Honda Accord. There he joins the queue to view, sits inside the car, tries out every single feature he can see – pulling down the sun visor, pushing in the cigarette lighter – until the Honda's alloted slot is over, and it's time to make his way to NGK Spark Plugs (UK) Ltd.

Another Car Man is The Big Boy. The Car Show is enormous, filling cavernous halls with stalls, stages, cars, people, people, people – but Big Boy takes his time, strolling around the venue, moseying over to the newest, biggest Beemer, the flashest Aston, Ferrari, Porsche. He always ends up in the Products and Services arena, at Fone Bitz, or Blaupunkt, or Sly Fox, who make radar detectors, so you can drive without fear of sneaky speed camera flashes. Big Boy also spends quite some time in front of the dancing girls.

What do you mean, you didn't know about the dancing girls? There's loads of them at the Car Show, employed to prance about in spangly leotards before particular vehicles (and before you come over funny, there's dancing boys, too. Who says feminism's had not effect?) At last year's Car Show, there were dancers of both sexes dancing the concept of the Citroën Xsara, pointing their toes 'to indicate that the Xsara is available in three stunning body styles, coupé, five-door hatchback and estate, each with superb levels of equipment and specification and all beautifully style'. The dancers showed us this by wearing yellow and making like an ocean, all wavy arms and curved backs.

Another Car Man? How about Car Dad? Car Dad has come along with his teenage son in an effort to bond. Son was OK with this. A few hours ago. Now Son is getting desperate, hanging back, looking for the burger bar, deciding that he needs the toilet RIGHT NOW. You see, Son thought he'd be on a Big Boy run, checking out the motors that matter. Instead, Car Dad has spent all day at the Classic Car stall, mooning his lost, free youth and ignoring the living embodiment of it.

So now you know everything you need to about the Car Show. It just remains for me to tell you that at last year's, the Ford Focus was the absolute star of the whole palaver. Ford's stand (a strange metal bridge over a gurgling water feature) was completely packed, with Schedules and Big Boys and Car Dads and everyone else. All had come to see the Focus. The Focus, back then, looked pretty wild for a Ford. OK, there'd been the bonkers Ford Ka and the growly Puma: but, compared with the popular standards of the Ford fleet – the Mondeo, the Fiesta – the Focus appeared outrageous. A car aimed squarely at the mass market, a family runaround, a mainstream, well-priced, meat-and-two veg vehicle that looked like a concept car. Its shape was modern: its back, in particular, was utterly distinctive, with its segmented lights and curved lines. It was best in silver, like a Merc. I thought: what a fantastic vision – it'll never sell. We British are a conservative lot, when it comes to cars. Nothing too flash. You don't want it keyed when you leave it in a multistorey.

But then I actually got to dive a Focus. And I instantly changed my mind. The Focus is a world-beater. It will sell and sell. It's a brilliant, brilliant car. Practically designed – shockingly economical; plus you can fit five adults in without complaint – but also a wonderful drive. The key, for me, was the gearstick. Metal to the touch – none of those horrible slipabout covers – it slid into gear with a light, joyous click that I could recall for days afterwards. I had the Zetec version, so the engine was cute and fiery (burning off at traffic lights is particularly gratifying when you're driving what looks like one step down from a people carrier).

You could tell it was a good 'un: it satisfied every Car Man rolled into one. Schedule Head would love the sensibleness, Big Boy the tuning, and Car Dad – well, Car Dad would have no choice but to invest. You can't fit a family of four into an MGB.

Ford Focus *Zetec Ghia*	
Price	£14,500
Insurance group	6E
MPG	40.9
Engine	1.6-litre 16v
Driven wheels	Front
Power(bhp)	100
Max speed (mph)	115
0–60 (secs)	10.9

The key, for me, was the gearstick. Metal to the touch – none of those horrible slipabout covers

The presentational features of a text will change according to its audience and purpose. For example, writing for small children usually has large pictures, bold print and very few words. Texts aimed at adults generally have fewer pictures, smaller print and more words.

Now that you have learned about audience, purpose and presentation, you are ready to write some of your own non-fiction texts.

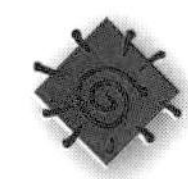

Activity 5 WS ICT

Write and design each of the following:

a a birthday card for a younger brother, sister or cousin
- Pictures and a birthday message are important here.
- You need use only a few words.

b instructions for looking after a pet
- You will need to write out your instructions in list form.
- You may want to use pictures as well.

c a poster advertising a sporting event or a concert in your school
- You will need to give details of the date, time and place.
- How much will you charge for the tickets?

Before you begin, think about these questions:
- Who are you writing for?
- Do you need to use pictures?
- What sort of pictures will you need and where will you place them in the text?
- Where do you need to place your information on the page?
- Do you need to use a lot of words or just a few?

You can draw attention to the words by:
- using **bold** headings
- using CAPITAL letters for some important words
- using different sizes of writing and type
- using handwriting to make the information more personal.

14 Formal and informal language

This unit will help you to:
- **decide when to write in an informal way**
- **decide when to write in a formal way**
- **learn how to write in different forms, including letters and e-mails.**

Formal or informal?

When we write, our language changes according to the person or people we are writing for. Most of us do this automatically when we are speaking. Without really thinking, we adopt a different tone of voice and use different words when talking, for example, to our friends and our teachers.

When writing to people you know well, you will probably use the same kind of words that you would use if you were speaking to them. You might use slang and shorten your words. You might also tend to use short and simple sentences. These are both signs of informal language.

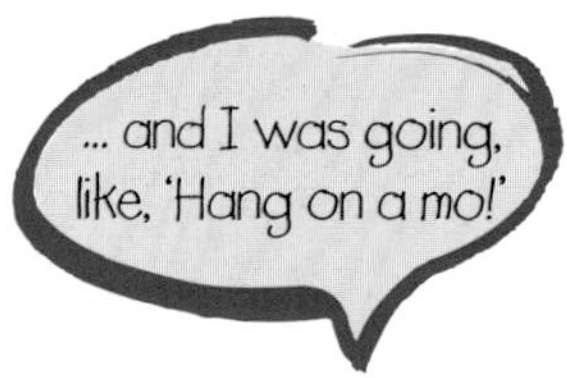

You need to use a formal language like in the example below when:
- you write to someone you don't know very well
- you need to write in polite terms
- you are writing for business.

Dear Mr Denman
I am writing to apply for the post of service reception clerk, advertised in the Gazette of 24 November.

Now look at the examples opposite:

TEXT A

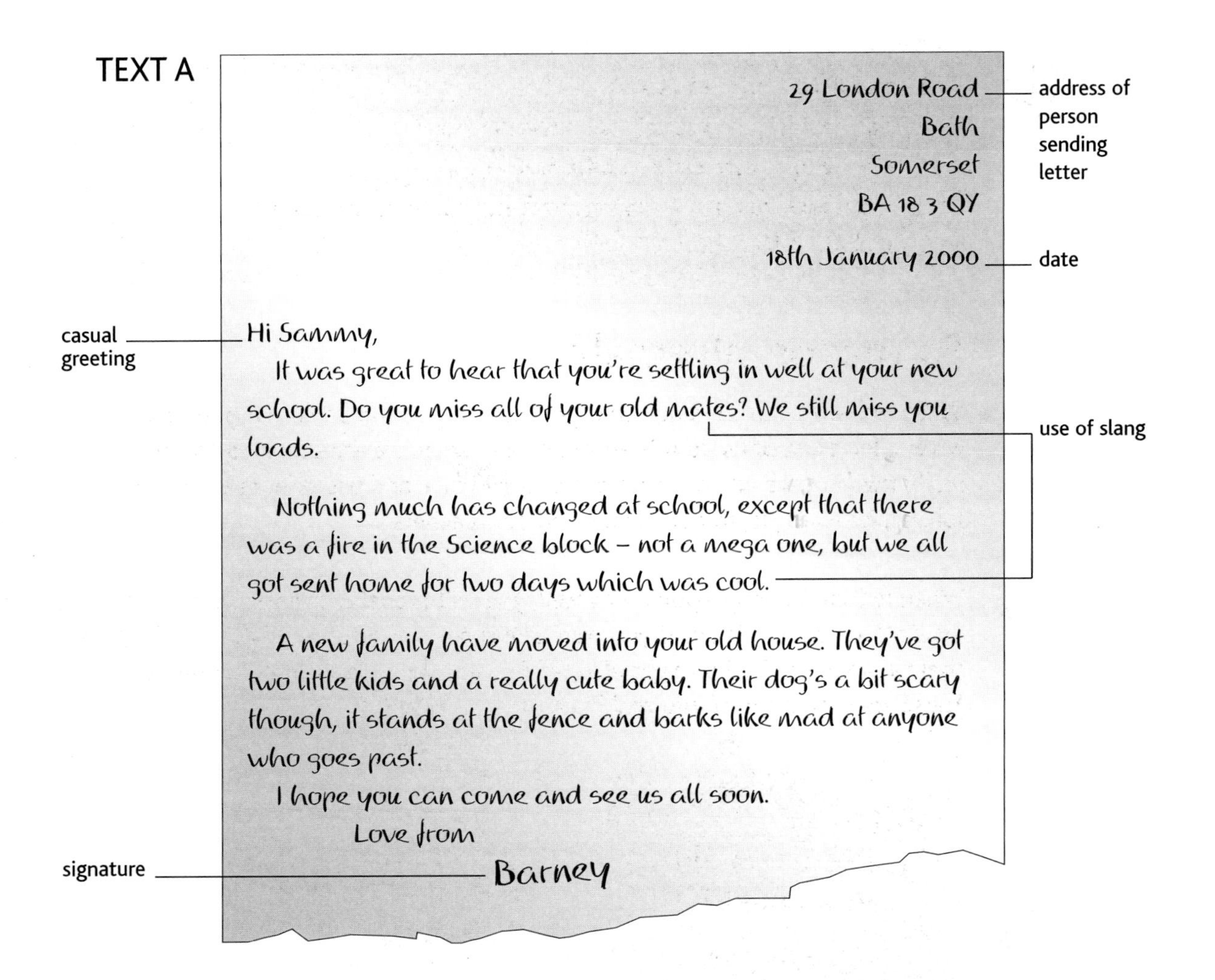
29 London Road
Bath
Somerset
BA 18 3 QY

18th January 2000

Hi Sammy,

It was great to hear that you're settling in well at your new school. Do you miss all of your old mates? We still miss you loads.

Nothing much has changed at school, except that there was a fire in the Science block – not a mega one, but we all got sent home for two days which was cool.

A new family have moved into your old house. They've got two little kids and a really cute baby. Their dog's a bit scary though, it stands at the fence and barks like mad at anyone who goes past.

I hope you can come and see us all soon.

Love from

Barney

TEXT B

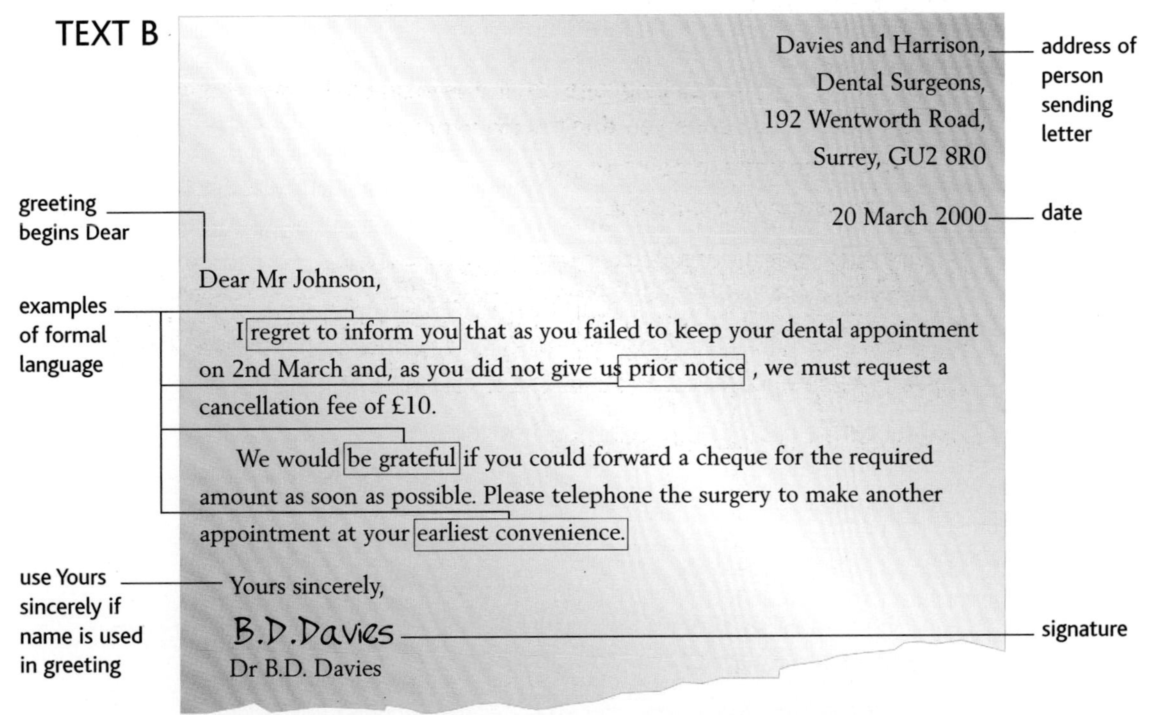
Davies and Harrison,
Dental Surgeons,
192 Wentworth Road,
Surrey, GU2 8R0

20 March 2000

Dear Mr Johnson,

I regret to inform you that as you failed to keep your dental appointment on 2nd March and, as you did not give us prior notice, we must request a cancellation fee of £10.

We would be grateful if you could forward a cheque for the required amount as soon as possible. Please telephone the surgery to make another appointment at your earliest convenience.

Yours sincerely,

B.D.Davies

Dr B.D. Davies

Activity 1

Discuss the letters on page 123 with a partner and decide which is informal and which is formal. Write down your answer, explaining how you made your decision. The following clues will help you:

- use of slang
- use of long words with difficult meanings
- use of shortened forms of words
- use of short sentences.

Ask yourself the following questions:

- Does the writer know the reader personally?
- Is the overall tone friendly or polite?

Activity 2 

You ordered a spell from the following advertisement in your local newspaper:

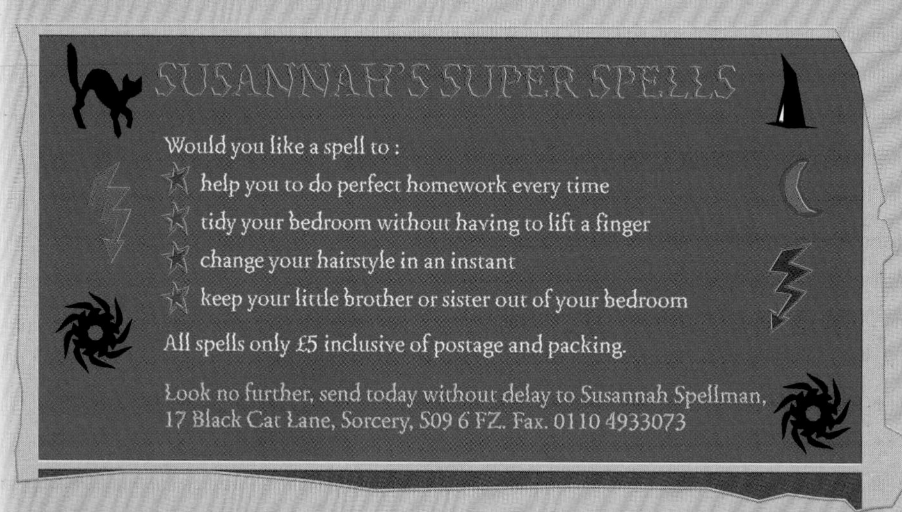

SUSANNAH'S SUPER SPELLS
Would you like a spell to :
help you to do perfect homework every time
tidy your bedroom without having to lift a finger
change your hairstyle in an instant
keep your little brother or sister out of your bedroom
All spells only £5 inclusive of postage and packing.
Look no further, send today without delay to Susannah Spellman,
17 Black Cat Lane, Sorcery, S09 6 FZ. Fax. 0110 4933073

It is now three weeks since you received your spell and you are not at all satisfied. Perhaps your hair turned bright blue when you used the spell for changing your hairstyle or perhaps all of your shoes disappeared when your bedroom was tidied for you.

Write a formal letter of complaint to Susannah Spellman, explaining to her that you are not pleased with the spell and would like your money back.

Key words and phrases: I regret, most dissatisfied, unfortunate effect, embarrassed, foolish, demand, without delay, I would be grateful, I cannot recommend.

Activity 3

Write a letter to a friend telling him or her what happened the day the spell went wrong.

This is an informal letter.

E-mails

Another way of sending messages is by e-mail.

An e-mail is electronic mail which you send on computer. Usually the purpose of e-mail is to send a short message instantly. The tone can be formal or informal, but because the message is usually short, the wording is like on a postcard. This means using short sentences or phrases.

If you were to send an e-mail to a friend in London asking him to meet you at the station, your message might look like the one below. As you can see, the tone is informal because this e-mail is being sent by one friend to another.

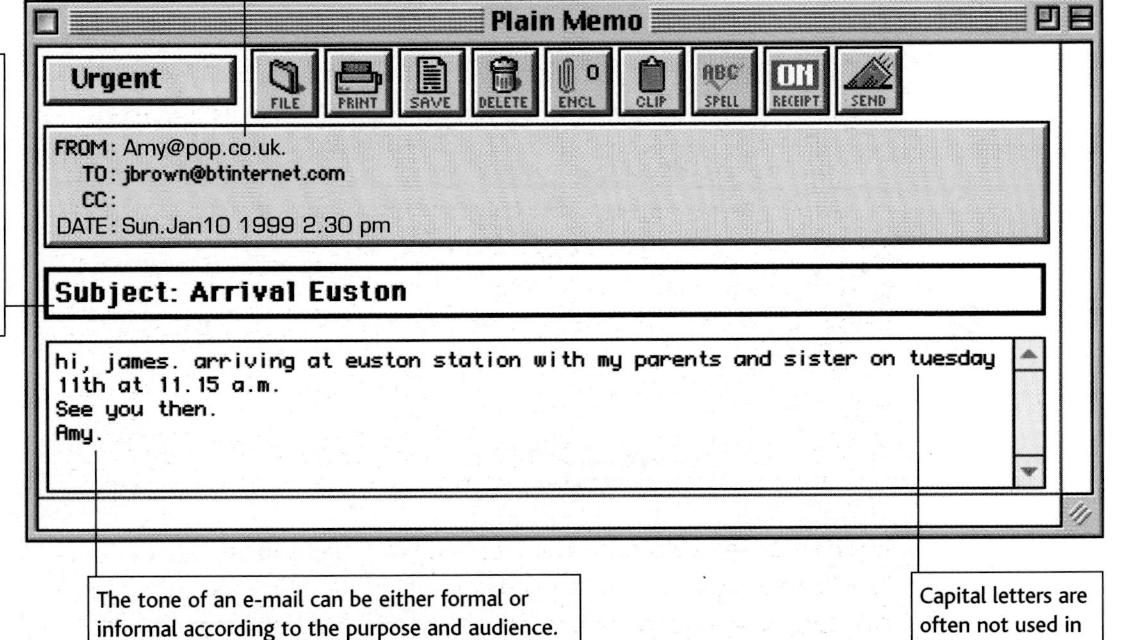

E-mail addresses do not look like ordinary addresses. This is because the message is sent on a computer and the words 'pop' and 'btinternet' refer to the companies which are used to send and receive the messages.
Plain Memo
Urgent
FILE
PRINT
SAVE
DELETE
ENCL
CLIP
SPELL
RECEIPT
SEND
FROM: Amy@pop.co.uk.
TO: jbrown@btinternet.com
CC:
DATE: Sun.Jan10 1999 2.30 pm
Subject: Arrival Euston
hi, james. arriving at euston station with my parents and sister on tuesday 11th at 11.15 a.m.
See you then.
Amy.
The topic or subject of your message is given before the message itself so that people in a hurry can read it very quickly.
The tone of an e-mail can be either formal or informal according to the purpose and audience.
Capital letters are often not used in e-mail messages.

Activity 4 WS ICT

Now write your own e-mail message to your French pen-friend in Paris. Ask her to meet you at Charles de Gaulle Airport. Her name is Danielle. Remember to copy the layout of the message above. You can use the same e-mail addresses as above. If you do not have access to e-mail, write your message out by hand.

Activity 5

Answer the following questions with either F for formal or I for informal.

1 You begin a letter with the words 'Hi, how's it going?' Is this a formal or an informal opening?

2 You end a letter with the words 'Yours sincerely'. Is this a formal or an informal ending?

3 You write a letter applying for a Saturday job in your local newsagent's. Is this a formal or an informal letter?

4 You write a letter which includes the words 'I regret to inform you'. Is this a formal or an informal letter?

5 You write a letter to a new pen-friend. Would you use a formal or an informal style?

6 You receive a letter from a travel company informing you that you have won a holiday to America. Is this a formal or an informal letter?

7 You receive a letter from your Head Teacher which confirms the dates of the school holidays. Is this a formal or an informal letter?

8 You write a letter to the problem page of a magazine for teenagers. Would you use formal or informal language?

9 You send an e-mail to a friend who is now living abroad. Is this formal or informal?

10 You send an e-mail to order goods quickly. Is this formal or informal?

15 Organising your ideas

This unit will help you to:
- **draft and re-draft your work**
- **write reports**
- **write clear instructions and directions**
- **give explanations and advice.**

Reports are usually written to inform readers of events which have taken place. They are written in the past tense because they deal with things which have already happened by the time we read about them. (For more information on the past tense, turn to page 169.)

Reports can take a number of different forms.

Newspaper reports

Newspaper reports are written to tell people about what has happened in the world or in a particular local area.

They are designed to give as much information as possible in quite a small space and to answer the following questions:

- WHO?
- WHAT?
- WHEN?
- WHERE?
- WHY?
- HOW?

In order to attract the attention of readers they have headlines written in **bold** type.

The first paragraph of the story is often also in bold type. It contains the main points, and then the rest of the story gives further details.

Read the story on the next page to help you understand how a newspaper report is written.

Some of the words spoken by the people involved have been included. These words are known as **direct speech**. They have been put into the article to show how the people at the scene reacted at the time. The use of direct speech makes the reader feel they were actually there.

JUMBO CAUSES CHAOS IN CITY CENTRE

■ YESTERDAY midday traffic came to a standstill in the centre of Manchester when an elephant escaped from a circus van and took a stroll in Market Street.

The elephant, known as Cindy, had escaped from a van belonging to Brown's Circus which was travelling through the city centre on its way to a local park. While shoppers, businessmen and circus workers tried in vain to catch her, 3-year-old Cindy lumbered between cars waiting at traffic lights.

Cindy, who did not appear to be disturbed by the shouts of passers-by and the tooting of car horns, decided to take a rest and sat down on the bonnet of a BMW belonging to solicitor Richard Johnson. 'I was rather alarmed, I thought my car was going to be crushed,' he said.

Keepers from a nearby zoo managed to lead Cindy away whilst the police sorted out the chaos caused by the traffic jams which had built up. 'I've never seen anything like it before. I'm glad no-one was hurt,' Police Constable Jane Richardson told our reporter.

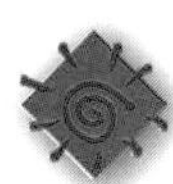

Activity 1

Read the newspaper article above.

1 Make a list of information from the story which answers these questions:

- **a** Who is it about?
- **b** What happened?
- **c** When did it happen?
- **d** Where did it happen?
- **e** Why did it happen?
- **f** How was it solved?

2 We are also given information about the feelings of two of the people involved in this incident. In your own words, write down how the solicitor and the police officer felt.

For more information on direct speech and how to write it down, turn to pages 93–99.

Making notes

Like the newspaper reporter, the police constable who was first at the scene would also have had to write a report. The police constable's notes would have looked very like those of the newspaper reporter, but the report would probably have been slightly different. It would have looked something like this:

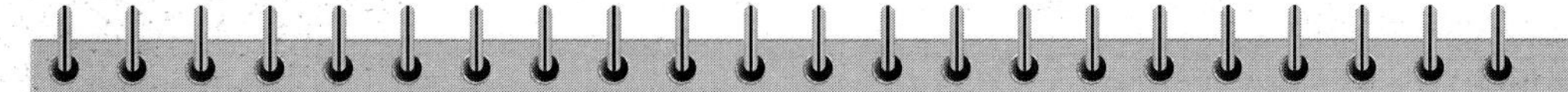

Yesterday at 12.05.pm I received a call on my radio giving details about a traffic incident in Market Street.

On arriving at the scene, I observed an elephant moving in and out of traffic. There were traffic jams as drivers were unwilling to drive into the path of the elephant.The elephant sat on the car bonnet of a BMW car, number S841 ROU, owned by Mr. R. Johnson.

I radioed for help to Sutton Zoo and keepers arrived at 12.25pm. They were able to rescue the elephant and lead it away into a circus van. All traffic jams were cleared by 12.50.pm and traffic was flowing freely again.

Later today I shall be interviewing the owner of Brown's Circus and Mr. R.Johnson.

Signed Date

Although the police constable's report deals with exactly the same incident as the newspaper story there are differences in the way each is written and presented. Both reports are written with the same purpose – to inform – but they are written for different **audiences**. This means that each writer uses a different type of language to explain what happened.

Activity 2 ICT

Read the newspaper story and the police report again.

Work with a partner to see how many differences you can spot.

Write down a list of the differences under the following headings:

Type of language: formal or informal?
Use of precise times
Descriptions of people
Descriptions of feelings

Make sure you include examples from each article.

Writing reports

In a report you should:

- make sure your report gives clear information
- choose the right sort of language for the type of report you are writing

Remember that reports for newspapers begin with headlines. They also often use some direct speech to interest their readers.

Read the accounts below which give details of the sighting of a strange object in the sky above the village of Enderby. Then complete the activities that follow:

MRS HALLIWELL'S ACCOUNT

I was just putting my daughter Emily to bed, it must have been about seven o'clock because we'd just finished watching that cartoon programme with the snakes in it. Do you know the one I mean? Anyway, she looked out of the window to say goodnight to the moon, she likes doing that, you know. Then she screamed and screamed – I thought she'd hurt herself or something.

When I looked out I saw this huge round thing in the sky with flashing lights and a sort of TV aerial on top. It had little windows in and through one of the little windows I could see a face peering out at me. It had a small head with big eyes and it was laughing.

That's when I fainted. When I came round my husband and little girl were standing over me. My husband said there was nothing there and I must have been imagining it, but I know I wasn't.

RORY BREWSTER'S ACCOUNT

I was on my way to my mate's house on my bike when I heard a funny noise in the sky. At first I thought it must be one of those low-flying planes, they can really scare you sometimes. Then I looked up and I saw this huge shiny round thing in the sky.

It was made out of shiny stuff and it had a thing turning round on the top.

At first I was that scared I didn't do anything, I just gawped at it. That's when I saw the windows and them little faces. There were people looking out of the windows smiling at me. They had little heads and great big eyes, but they weren't frightening, really. I think I saw three of them.

HAROLD PEACOCK'S ACCOUNT

I was just about to watch the seven o'clock news when I heard a rather peculiar noise outside my window. When I opened the curtains to investigate I was astounded. There in the sky was what looked just like a spaceship from a children's comic or something. It was travelling very slowly and appeared to be looking for something. I wasn't worried at all, just rather fascinated. Wouldn't you have been?

The spaceship, I don't know what else to call it, had these little portholes like on a real ship. I could see very clearly that there were people inside, well sort of people, they had huge eyes and somehow they looked friendly. I thought they might have been waving to me.

I went to call my wife, I knew she'd be interested too, but when I brought her to the window they'd gone. A shame really.

Activity 3 ICT

1 These accounts vary. Each of the three eyewitnesses noticed something slightly different. How many differences can you spot?

2 Each of the three eyewitnesses felt differently about the appearance of the spaceship. What were their feelings?

3 These accounts sound as if the people are talking directly to us. The accounts have been written down using the actual words they used. How many examples can you find of words and phrases which are more likely to be used in conversation than in writing?

Remember that the language of reports is usually formal English, except for newspaper reports when you use direct speech to write down the actual words someone has said.

Activity 4

Imagine that you are the local police constable. You have to write a report for your sergeant on the strange sightings in the sky. Follow these stages:

- Make notes on all of the witnesses' statements. Remember that notes are written in a shortened form. They are never written in full sentences.
- Organise your notes in the right order so that you can write a clear report. Use the following headings to help you:

  Time of sighting
  Place of sighting
  Number of sightings
  Details of spaceship and people on board
- When writing your report use the note headings to help you to organise your work into paragraphs. Include all the notes under each heading in one paragraph.
- Remember this is a formal report.

Key words and phrases: observed, sighted, approximately, appeared to be.

Activity 5 WS

Now you are going to use your notes to write a first draft of a newspaper report of the spaceship sightings in Enderby. This time your purpose is not just to inform readers, it is also to interest and entertain them.

Your newspaper report should include the following:

- an eye-catching headline
- an opening paragraph summarising the main points of the story
- further details of the sighting of the spaceships, including the people who saw them and their reactions
- some direct speech using the actual words of the people involved.

Drafting

A draft is a first attempt at a piece of work. It gives you the chance to look at your work carefully to see what improvements can be made.

Look at the newspaper article you wrote in Activity 5. Begin by looking again at the checklist. Have you included everything on the list? If not, now is the time to make some additions. Perhaps you think your headline is not dramatic enough. You can change it.

Perhaps you have included too many of the words spoken by witnesses. You can cross some of them out.

Maybe you feel your report is not exciting enough to interest readers. You can change some of the words you have used and replace them with more dramatic and exciting words.

You may also want to change the order in which you have written things down.

The best way to make changes is by using a different coloured pen or pencil to write above or next to your first choice. You could also check your work with the person sitting next to you.

Once you have changed your first draft by writing alterations on your text, now it is time to produce your best version. Before you do this, check that you have used capital letters, full stops, commas and speech marks correctly. You should also check whether your spelling is correct.

Now that all of this has been done you are ready to produce a perfect newspaper report!

THE LOCAL NEWS

Aliens in Enderby!

Residents report sightings of extra-terrestrial visitors

Writing instructions

Everybody needs to read instructions. You find them all around you in everyday life. You will find instructions on how to operate household appliances such as toasters, video recorders and washing machines. Some of these instructions are written in quite complicated language because they are written for an adult audience. You may not have looked at them very closely before. Look around your house and see how many different sets of instructions you can find.

Some instructions you have probably read closely are the instructions you get when you buy a new computer or a new board game.

Look carefully at the instructions below, given for a children's game called Scaredy Cat.

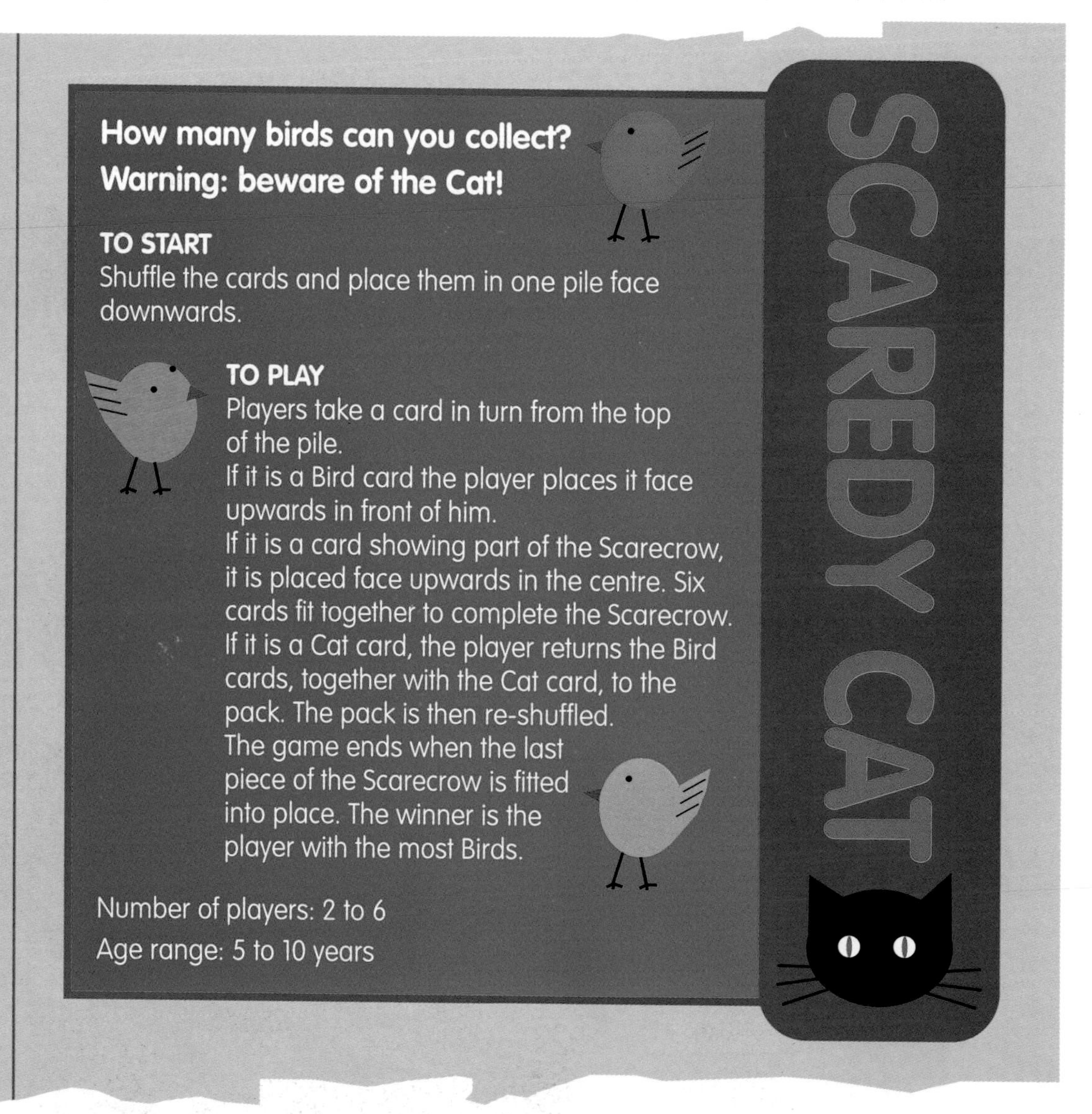

How many birds can you collect?
Warning: beware of the Cat!

TO START
Shuffle the cards and place them in one pile face downwards.

TO PLAY
Players take a card in turn from the top of the pile.
If it is a Bird card the player places it face upwards in front of him.
If it is a card showing part of the Scarecrow, it is placed face upwards in the centre. Six cards fit together to complete the Scarecrow.
If it is a Cat card, the player returns the Bird cards, together with the Cat card, to the pack. The pack is then re-shuffled.
The game ends when the last piece of the Scarecrow is fitted into place. The winner is the player with the most Birds.

Number of players: 2 to 6
Age range: 5 to 10 years

Have another look at the instructions and notice:

- the use of a question mark and the use of the word 'you' – this makes the reader feel they are being spoken to personally
- the use of an exclamation mark – this makes the game seem exciting
- the use of capital letters at the beginning of important parts in the instructions such as TO START and TO PLAY
- the use of bold type to draw attention to key phrases in the instructions
- the use of very short paragraphs to make the instructions easy to follow.

Sometimes when you are given instructions you want to have some questions answered. The questions have been answered by the sentences which begin with the word 'If'.

Can you work out what the questions were?

Activity 6

Choose a very simple game, perhaps a card game like Snap or Happy Families, and write a set of instructions for a younger child. You might prefer to write instructions for a game that you played in the playground when you were younger.

Remember to follow the model of the Scaredy Cat game explained above. Check the bullet points above to make sure that you have not left anything out. You might also want to include a picture to make your instructions look interesting and appealing to your audience.

When you are writing instructions it is very important that your readers can understand them. You should not write long and complicated sentences because this might confuse your audience rather than help them to understand what to do.

Look at the following instructions for a plastic repair kit.

VINYL PLASTIC REPAIR KIT

INSTRUCTIONS

1 Cut to required size depending on hole or puncture.
2 Thoroughly clean damaged surface and allow to dry for a minimum of 10 minutes.
3 Remove the vinyl patch from the paper backing.
4 Press patch firmly over hole or puncture.
5 Do not inflate for 20 minutes.

Notice the following points:

- the title has been written in capital letters
- the most important word – INSTRUCTIONS – has been written in capitals, bold print and has been underlined
- this time the instructions have been numbered because the order in which the instructions is followed is very important
- the instructions have been written out briefly in short, clear sentences.

Activity 7 ◆WS ◆ICT

Write a set of simple, clear instructions for making a cup of tea. Model these on the instructions for the plastic repair kit. Check the bullet points to make sure that your instructions are as clear as the ones above.

Sometimes it is useful to draw a diagram to help a reader follow your instructions.

Activity 8

Now design your own set of instructions using diagrams. You might want to explain how to do a particular trick with a yo-yo, or how to make a pop-up card. You may prefer to choose something of your own.

Look at the map on the right giving directions to the Blackpool Sea Life Centre.

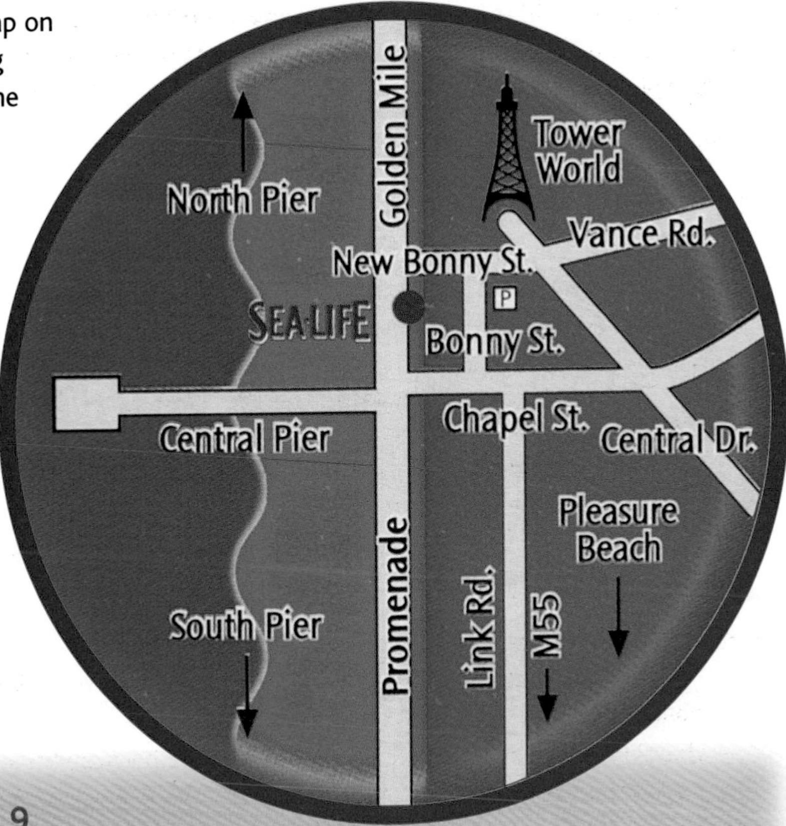

Activity 9

Imagine that you are on Central Drive coming from the direction of the Pleasure Beach. Someone asks you the way to the Sea Life Centre. Using the map, give them the directions they need.

If you are writing these directions out, remember to use full stops and capital letters. You can begin a new sentence for each part of the directions.

Activity 10 ICT

Choose a place that you know well in the centre of a town you visit often. Draw a simple map of the streets near to your chosen place. Include important landmarks such as other large buildings, perhaps a church or a hotel. You might include places like an ice-skating rink, a cinema or a swimming pool.

Once you have decided on your place and you have drawn your map, write a set of clear directions explaining how to get to it.

Key words and phrases: turn left/right, next, take, look.

These words are known as directives and you can read more about them in the Language in Action Section on page 174.

Assignment 4

Your Head of Year has asked you and a group of friends to organise an end-of-year trip to Camelot Theme Park. She has given you the brochure below.

You have been asked to produce the following:

- a poster advertising the trip
- a formal letter to parents informing them about the trip
- a letter to students giving them details and instructions about the trip
- a report on the trip for your Head of Year.

Before you begin to write, make notes on the attractions of Camelot under the following headings:

- ◆ rides
- ◆ live shows and attractions
- ◆ other attractions.

Remember to keep your notes short and to use your own words.

Designing the poster

Remember to include: the time and date of the trip, a few brief details about Camelot, details of who to contact for further information and pictures or designs to make your poster look interesting. Remember also to vary the size of your letters so that important details are emphasised.

Key words: attention, exciting, thrilling, unmissable

Letter to parents

This letter should be short and to the point. The tone should be formal.

Look back at page 123 for a reminder of how to end formal letters.

In your letter you should tell parents about the trip, the time and date of the trip including a time for the return to school, and details of how to pay.

Key words: information, departure, return, collect, payment, latest

Letter to other students in your year

This letter should give more detailed information explaining to students, in a friendly and informal tone, what sort of things they need to bring for the trip – packed lunch, snacks for the coach journey, personal stereo, etc.

You can also explain in more detail what sort of attractions students can expect. Remember to stress the enjoyable aspects.

Your final paragraph should include a reminder of what fun the trip will be.

Key words and phrases: don't miss it, opportunity, fun-packed

Report for your Head of Year after the trip

Look back at pages 130–131 to remind yourself how to write reports. This report should be written in clear, formal English (remember your audience is an adult).

You should write one paragraph on each of the following: the journey to and from Camelot, the highlights of the trip, details of any accidents and lost property and the behaviour of the students on the trip.

Key words: successful, punctual, rewarding, enjoyable, first aid, lost property office

Section C ◆ Speaking and listening
Introduction

Just as reading and writing are linked, so are speaking and listening. Although most of the focus in this unit is about speaking, the importance of careful listening should never be forgotten.

Many of the kinds of speaking you will do as you work through this unit involve an audience – usually the rest of the class. That requires some confidence and trust in the people you are speaking to, the listeners. Everybody stumbles sometimes when talking to an audience: it's practice which helps everyone improve. Listening is also something that can be practised.

You learned to talk before you learned to write. For most everyday communication you speak and listen to people. Most of the speaking is informal. If something is 'formal' it is probably planned. For example, a speech at a wedding or a talk in an assembly, would be planned in advance. Formal talk may also suggest some seriousness, though humour is something that livens up most talks. 'Informal', on the other hand, suggests 'everyday', so that chat, conversation and things like that are 'informal'.

As you work through this unit you will find yourself being asked to speak and listen in a range of different situations: sometimes you will be speaking imaginatively in role, sometimes you will be speaking from your own experience. You will be speaking on your own, in pairs and small groups.

Speaking and listening are not taken seriously as 'work' by some people. This is because most people feel that, having been speaking for years and years, they are experts and don't have to practise! The speaking and listening activities in this unit will help you realise that different situations need different kinds of speaking.

17 The difference between speaking and writing

This unit will help you to:
- **think about the differences between speaking and writing**
- **structure spoken stories in different ways**
- **listen to a variety of speech.**

You learned to talk before you learned to write. For most everyday communication you speak and listen to people. Most of the speaking is informal. If something is 'formal' it is probably planned.

Writing tends to be more formal than speaking. Writing is usually organised into sentences and paragraphs with punctuation to mark out pauses and emphasize meaning.

But some writing is 'informal'. Notes, for example, are quite informal. Look at this one:

Mum. 6.00 Thurs.
At Kev's. Having tea there.
Back 8.00
Love ya

You've probably left a note like this for someone in your family.

You could do it very formally:

2 Station Road,
Sadtown,
Bumbleshire.

Thursday, 1st September

Dear Mother,

At time of writing it is six o'clock.

I would just like you to know that I am going round to Kevin's house. Kevin's mother has said she will make tea for us. I will be back home at eight o'clock.

With love,

A formal piece of writing, turning the note into a letter, just wouldn't seem appropriate.

If you are asked to write an essay or a story you will end up with something that is formal: it has been planned and shaped. But on the way to writing it you might have:
- scribbled/jotted down/listed some rough ideas
- brainstormed ideas using things like spider diagrams.

These kinds of writing are informal.

Activity 1

Look at the examples below. Decide what you think the situation is, and whether the speech is formal or informal:

1 Good morning, everyone. This morning I would like us all to think about what we can do to help the refugees in Kosovo. I am sure you will have seen the pictures on your television screens of the terrible situation the refugees have found themselves in. There are three things I would like us to consider ...

2 Hello ... is that Mike? ... Oh, I'm sorry ... Oh ... Do you know when ...? ... Six? ... Yes, please ... Yes, that would be great ... Bye.

3 It's well good. It's like, sort of a lift thing and they strap you in at the bottom – it takes three of you. You go up about ... I don't know really ... it's about, I don't know, about 200 feet it must be. Then they stop it at the top and then, wham! you just go rocketing down.

4 Latest reports suggest that up to sixty people have died in what has become one of the worst storms to hit this remote island.

5 **a** I'd like to ask you about your previous employment. Could you tell me, please, why you left there?

b Well, there were two reasons really. I felt I had gone as far as I could in that particular position. I needed a new challenge. And, secondly, I have always had an interest in what you are achieving here.

6 **a** Hiya.
b All right?
a How d'ya get on?
b Great. Four nil. We murdered 'em.

Thinking about these examples and your own knowledge, what do you think are the main differences between informal and formal speech?

Activity 2

Copy and complete the table below giving the main features of formal and informal speech. You will need to add more rows.

INFORMAL TALK	FORMAL TALK
Slang	Standard English
Incomplete sentences	

Have you ever thought about the differences between speaking and writing? Sometimes you have a choice between the two. If you had an argument with your friend and the two of you ended up not talking to each other for a while, you might decide you want to do something about it. You could:

- write them a note
- telephone them
- decide to talk to them face to face.

Activity 3

With a partner, talk through the advantages and disadvantages of each of these methods. What problems might there be in each case?

METHODS	ADVANTAGES	DISADVANTAGES
write them a note		
telephone them		
talk to them face to face		

Narrating

We spend a lot of time telling and listening to stories. Stories appear in many different forms in different media:

novels	films	soaps	cartoons	photo-stories
short stories	conversations	television news	newspaper articles	jokes
plays	interviews	dramas	poems	adverts
picture books	songs	photographs	pictures	reports

Telling stories seems to come more naturally to some people than to others, but it is something we can all learn about.

Anecdotes

Anecdotes are short accounts of something that has happened. They are often quite funny. We use a lot of anecdotes in everyday conversation:

'I can't come out tonight; my mum says I've got to stay in to tidy my bedroom. She went up there on Saturday morning to get my dirty washing and found a plate covered with something she thought was alive! It was the remains of the burgers you and I ate up there two weeks ago! She says I'm grounded till the place is spotless!'

That's a little story that's being used to explain something to a friend. We use anecdotes like this all the time almost without thinking about it.

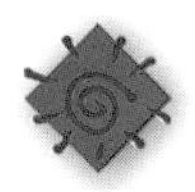

Activity 4

1 **Work with a partner.** Take it in turns to tell three or four short true stories about some of the different things that have happened to you recently. Think about things that have been funny, embarrassing, strange, worrying, unusual. You should only share stories that you feel comfortable about because the rest of the class might be going to hear one of them. As you listen to each other, try to decide which of the anecdotes you have been told is the most interesting.

2 **Share with the class.** Around the class take it in turns to share one of the anecdotes you have been told. You won't be telling the class your own story, you will be telling them one that has been told to you. This should test out how well you have listened to your partner!

Anecdotes don't really take much shaping. They are usually quite easy to tell because there isn't much background or detail to fill in. Longer stories will need a little more thought and may come out in a variety of ways.

Interviews

Sometimes a story can be brought out of someone by asking them good questions.

Activity 5 WS ICT

Work in pairs.

A local radio station wants to feature more stories about the younger people in its area. It is inviting 11–12 year old students to send in mini-interviews about themselves and the lives they lead. The interviews need to fit into schedules and must therefore be exactly three minutes long. Read through the steps below to help you prepare.

Preparation

One of you needs to be the interviewer and the other the person being interviewed. Once you've got one interview ready, you need to change places and prepare the other one.

Stage 1: In only three minutes you can't tell a whole life story, so what the interviewer is trying to find out is something 'interesting', that will entertain a radio audience. Listeners especially like stories, so it is a good idea to try to uncover some interesting anecdotes.

You could ask questions about:

- family
- school
- embarrassing stories
- hobbies
- holidays
- likes/dislikes
- pets
- funny stories
- food.

Good questions will get more than one-word answers. If you ask a question and the answer is 'Yes' or 'No', it probably wasn't a very good question in the first place.

Stage 2: Once you've spent a bit of time talking decide the most interesting thing to focus on then you can begin to shape your interview.

You might decide to give your interview a clear structure from the beginning, for example:

- a factual introduction (date of birth, place of birth, family details)
- a few questions about the main topic of the interview
- a winding up and thank you.

Stage 3: Once you've got some idea of the shape of your interview, you need to rehearse it and time it. You'll find out if you need to add material or, as is more likely, cut some out.

Stage 4: Carry out your interview. Depending on the circumstances in your classroom, you could either record it on to audiotape or perform it in front of the class.

Telling stories

Read the following poem in pairs. It is the story of a student telling a teacher why he is late. One of you should take the part of the teacher and the other plays Blenkinsopp, the student.

Conversation Piece

Late again Blenkinsopp?
What's the excuse this time?
Not my fault sir.
Whose fault is it then?
5 *Grandma's sir.*
Grandma's. What did she do?
She died sir.
Died?
She's seriously dead all right sir.
10 That makes four grandmothers this term
And all on P. E. days Blenkinsopp.
I know. It's very upsetting sir.
How many grandmothers have you got
Blenkinsopp?
15 *Grandmothers sir? None sir.*
You said you had four.
All dead sir.
And what about yesterday Blenkinsopp?
What about yesterday sir?
20 You were absent yesterday.
That was the dentist sir.
The dentist died?
No sir. My teeth sir.
You missed the maths test Blenkinsopp.
25 *I'd been looking forward to it sir.*
Right, line up for P. E.
Can't sir.
No such word as 'can't' Blenkinsopp.
No kit sir.
30 Where is it?
Home sir.
What's it doing at home?
Not ironed sir.
Couldn't you iron it?
35 *Can't sir.*
Why not?
Bad hand sir.
Who usually does it?
Grandma sir.
40 Why couldn't she do it?
Dead sir.

Gareth Owen

Activity 6 WS ICT

Work with a partner to create your own conversation piece.

You need to come up with a flimsy excuse for being absent or late or not handing in homework, told in a way that makes it sound convincing. One of you will need to be the teacher while the other is the student.

To make it entertaining, the excuse should be far-fetched but with just enough detail to almost persuade us that it is real. Try to come up with your own ideas but some of the following might help:

'It was the goldfish's fault ...'

'Well, it was just like the X Files, sir, you wouldn't believe it ...'

Telling stories for different audiences and purposes

How you tell a story will depend on who you are telling it to and why you are telling it. For example, you wouldn't expect a TV news story to begin 'Once upon a time ...'.

Read the following extract:

The Iron Woman

About half a mile away a birdwatcher was bent over a bittern's nest, holding a dead bittern and feeling the cold eggs on which the dead bird had been sitting. From his hide, only ten feet away, he had been watching this bird all day, waiting for the eggs to start hatching. He knew the chicks were already overdue. When those first quakes had come, shuddering his camera on its tripod, he had told himself they were distant quarry blastings. He had guessed the strange wailing must be some kind of factory siren. He knew there was a big factory outside the town, only two or three miles away. What else could such things be? And when that second booming wail had come, he had just seen something far more startling. He stared through his binoculars. Two big blowflies were inspecting the eyes of the bittern on the nest. With a shock, he realised the bird was dead. All day, and probably yesterday too, he had been watching a dead bird. This was more important than any noises. So he had waded out, and lifted the dead mother from her eggs. He was horrified. She was quite stiff.

And it was then, as he stood there, thinking that he must take this bird and her eggs to be examined by some scientist, to find out what had killed them, it was then that the third wail came, far louder than the earlier ones. At the same moment the marsh shook, like a vast jelly, and he thought: An earthquake! And maybe that's a siren's warning!

He had made his hide at the edge of some higher ground that stuck out into the marsh from the road. Big bushy willow trees behind him blocked his view of what had terrified the heron and the seagull. But he was alarmed enough by the idea of an earthquake. Cradling the cold eggs in one hand, with the dead bittern tucked under his arm, he collected his camera and returned to his car parked among the willows. As he opened the car door, another jolt shook it.

He drove out along grassy ruts on to the road, not far from the bridge where Lucy had stood watching the eel. As he turned right, towards the town, his eyes widened and his brain whirled. The swaying, lumpy, black tower, about a hundred yards ahead, close to the road, could not possibly be anything. Unless it was some structure for aerials, something to do with radar, maybe, draped in camouflage. Even when it moved, he still tried to explain it. Maybe it was a windmill, without arms, being moved – as they move whole houses in America. Or maybe some film company was making a film, a horror film; it could be, and that would account for the hideous noises too. He simply did not know what to think – so he went on driving towards it.

40 But when it stepped out on to the road directly in front of him, he jammed on his brakes.

This, he could see, was something new. This had come up all on its own out of the marsh mud. Clumps and tangles of reeds still slithered down its black length, with the slime. As it dawned on him what he was looking at, 45 his head seemed to freeze. That was his hair trying to stand on end. Tears of pure fear began to pour down his cheeks. But he was a photographer – and no true photographer ever misses a chance.

He bundled his camera with him out of the car, snatched off the lens cover, and bowed over the viewfinder.

50 Blackness filled it. He backed away, swinging the camera from side to side, trying to squeeze the whole huge shape into the frame. But even before he got it full length he saw, in his viewfinder, that it had picked up his car. Aghast, but also overjoyed, he took shot after shot as the great figure slammed his car down on to the 55 road, raised it high and slammed it down again, and again, and again, like somebody trying to beat the dust out of a heavy rug. The birdwatcher remembered, with a fleeting pang, the bittern's eggs. They had been nested in his cap on the 60 passenger seat. But he forgot them as he saw the paint and glass exploding, like steam, each time the car banged down on to the road. Doors flew off, wheels bounded into the reeds, and the mouth in the head opened. As the terrible siren wail came out of that mouth, the birdwatcher turned and ran.

*from **The Iron Woman** by Ted Hughes*

Activity 7 WS ICT

Choose one of the following ways to retell the story:

- Imagine you are the birdwatcher. You rush to the police station in a panic. They ask you to calm down and tell them what happened.
- A paired activity. The birdwatcher tells his friend about what happened. The friend thinks it's a bit far-fetched and doesn't believe him. The birdwatcher does his best to persuade him that it's all true.

18 Describing

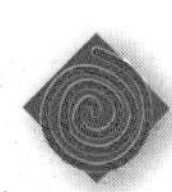

This unit will help you to:
- **describe things clearly**
- **consider different ways of describing things**
- **find the confidence to speak in a variety of situations.**

Activity 1 ICT

This activity will test how well you can describe details and how well your friends listen. You will need to be in groups of four or five.

On the next page there are twelve photographs of men's faces. Each of you, in turn, is going to choose one face to describe to the others in your group. They will have their books closed so that they cannot see the photographs. When you have finished, they will open their books, look at the faces and see if they can match one of them to your description.

Before you start, think about the following:
- What details can you describe that might be helpful
- the shape of the face, the nose, the mouth
- **colour** of eyes, hair, skin
- distinguishing features – anything that stands out
- your impressions – does the face look shifty, trustworthy, kind etc?

As a listener, how are you going to remember the details you are told? It would be a good idea to try to listen to key points – strong details which will help you tell one face from another.

Once everybody in your group has had a chance to describe one photograph, briefly discuss the descriptions.
- What worked?
- What caused difficulties?
- Does the order in which you describe things make any difference?
- Does the length of the description matter?

Activity 2

Imagine you are a witness to a crime. A gang of three men makes its getaway in a car. You see the men's faces. You are going to describe them to the police. Choose three faces from the page opposite to describe.

When you have finished your descriptions, the rest of the group should open their books, look at the faces and write down the three numbers they think match your descriptions.

1 2 3

4 5 6

7 8 9

10 11 12

On television, you can see things for yourself. You do not need a voiceover to tell you what is obvious. With radio it is different because you only have sounds. This next activity is about describing things clearly to a radio audience.

The small, uninhabited island of Mortonia has recently been visited by you and your group. This is an artist's impression of Mortonia:

You are going to make a five-minute radio programme in which you describe the island. The purpose is to entertain by sharing your thoughts on the unspoilt beauty of the island with your audience. You want to give an impression of a lovely landscape which should not be harmed by tourism or other development.

Activity 3 ICT

1 Work in groups of three or four. Before you look at the details of the island, spend a few minutes discussing the advantages and disadvantages of having to do this on radio. How would it be different were it on television or in a book or magazine? What are you going to have to do to make your description interesting?

2 Spend some time looking at the island. Discuss the different aspects you could describe. You'll have to use your imagination to fill in details. You need to think about how you are going to involve everyone in your group by giving them responsibility for a part of the programme. Here are some suggestions:

- You could each be given a particular part of the island to describe.
- You could each choose a different aspect of the island. One could look at wildlife; one could explore the river; another could look at the coast; someone could focus on the island at night.

You may be able to come up with your own structure.

3 Once you have sorted out a structure, you need to think about the details.

Don't just focus on what you can see. Think of the other things you can describe:

◆ sounds ◆ touch ◆ thoughts ◆ smells ◆ feelings.

4 You'll need to decide on a style. Will you imagine you are there on the island, with a tape recorder, recording your immediate impressions? Or do you want to imagine you are back home again and that your programme is based on notes and memories?

If you choose the first way, you might find yourself saying things like:

'This must be the most beautiful place on earth. I'm standing on a deserted, golden beach with the warm water lapping at my feet. Behind me are …'

Whereas the second way would be different:

'I spent a lot of time by the sea. The beach was a thin strip of golden sand. In the mornings when the tide went out I'd often find …'

5 Tape your programme if you possibly can. You could perhaps include sound effects like bird and animal sounds. You could also add some other imaginative touches: for example, if you had just climbed a mountain and were tape-recording your impressions, you might be a little out of breath.

Activity 4 WS

Make a presentation on your own.

Describe to the class a person who is important to you. Your talk should last a maximum of two minutes. You can choose from a variety of people:

- a relative – your mum or dad, perhaps
- a friend – one you have now or, perhaps, a friend from when you were younger
- a famous person you look up to or admire
- a person from history
- a character from a book.

Before you choose your subject, you need to think about the following:

- What kind of approach will make my talk interesting?
- What am I prepared to share with my audience and what do I wish to keep private?

Planning

1 Your talk must have a shape – you can't just stand up and start chatting. You need to break it down into different sections.
You might like to think about some of the following aspects:

- a physical description of the person: what they look like; what they wear
- a description of their mannerisms/personality/behaviour
- how they are important to you
- an anecdote that might help to bring your subject to life for an audience.

2 You need to think about whether you'll begin by telling your audience who the person is, or whether you want to delay telling them until the very end – it could come as a surprise to find out that the person they thought was your mum is actually a character from a cartoon!

3 Once you have chosen your subject and thought about the kind of things you want to say, you need to prepare your talk.

If your audience is a fairly large group of people, it helps to have eye contact with them when you are talking. This is because it helps them relate to you.

Try to avoid reading a script word for word. It would be better to have an outline and some prompt cards you can use. Opposite is an example of some prompt cards used by one student who was talking about her baby brother.

1.
He's lovely looking:
chubby
hair
bright clothes

2.
Personality:
Noisy
Happy when ..
Miserable when ...

3.
Some of the things he gets up to:
The dog anecdote
The wedding anecdote

4.
Why I love him:
He needs looking after
END: He's my baby brother and he's very important to me.

In America, many years ago, a national panic was caused by a radio programme. A young director was producing a radio version of a book called *The War of the Worlds*. The story is about a Martian invasion of earth. To make his radio drama interesting and believable the director began the drama as though it were a news broadcast. Thousands of Americans, hearing the 'news' and thinking it was true, panicked and fled from their homes. This incident shows the power of radio.

Activity 5 ICT

Prepare a short radio talk on one of the following imaginary scenarios:

- You are an astronaut. You have landed on Mars. You radio back what you can see.
- You have landed on a new planet. A strange creature is approaching you. You broadcast back what you can see.

- You are a radio reporter. You have heard stories about UFOs locally and you have gone to investigate. You set up your recording equipment and then a UFO appears. Describe what you see.
- You are a radio reporter. You have been asked by your boss to go and investigate a 'haunted house' story. You don't really believe in ghosts, but just as the clock strikes twelve you see something ...
- You are a radio reporter. There have been sightings of a strange beast in the local woods. Your boss asks you to go and investigate. You start to describe the wood and what you can see when suddenly something moves in the undergrowth ...

19 Explaining

This unit will help you to:
- **find ways to use language precisely**
- **listen carefully**
- **consider how best to use language suitable for your audience.**

If you explain something you are making it clearer and easier to understand.

Activity 1

Below is a list of 'difficult' words in English. Look up these words in a dictionary. Make sure of their meanings and then explain them to the class. You might think about:

- writing them on the board
- using hand-outs
- making posters
- giving examples
- using **mnemonics** or other learning tools.

1 Explain the difference between *effect* and *affect*.
2 Explain the difference between *there / their / they're*.
3 Explain the difference between *dependent* and *dependant*.
4 Explain the difference between *a lot* and *allot*.
5 Explain how to spell words beginning *dis–*, such as *disappear / disappoint / dislike / dissatisfaction*.
6 Explain the difference between *its* and *it's*.
7 Explain what **homophones** are. Give examples and tips on how to remember the differences between them.
8 Explain what a **suffix** is and what some of the most common ones are.
9 Explain what a **prefix** is and what some of the most common ones are.

Once you've completed this activity and listened to others, discuss which talks were the clearest and why.

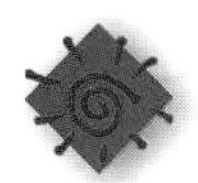

Activity 2

Work in pairs. There are two origami diagrams, A and B, below and on the next page. One of you should choose A and the other B.
Make your chosen origami model so that you know how to do it. Once you've made it, unfold again. Now you're ready to explain how to do it.

1 Whoever is A will begin. Your task is to explain to B how to make origami model A, following the numbered stages in your diagram. Your partner will have a piece of card or paper and will do only what you tell them.

2 Then change places, so that B can explain to A.

3 When you have both finished, talk about what was helpful and what was not.

A

BOAT *Use a square of paper*

1 fold here fold — first crease along the middle

2 fold in half — here fold

3 like this — now fold the two corners up

22

BOAT *continued*

4 like this — fold here

5 fold behind

6 and behind — fold down

7 like this — crease along marked lines and flatten bottom

the boat

23

B

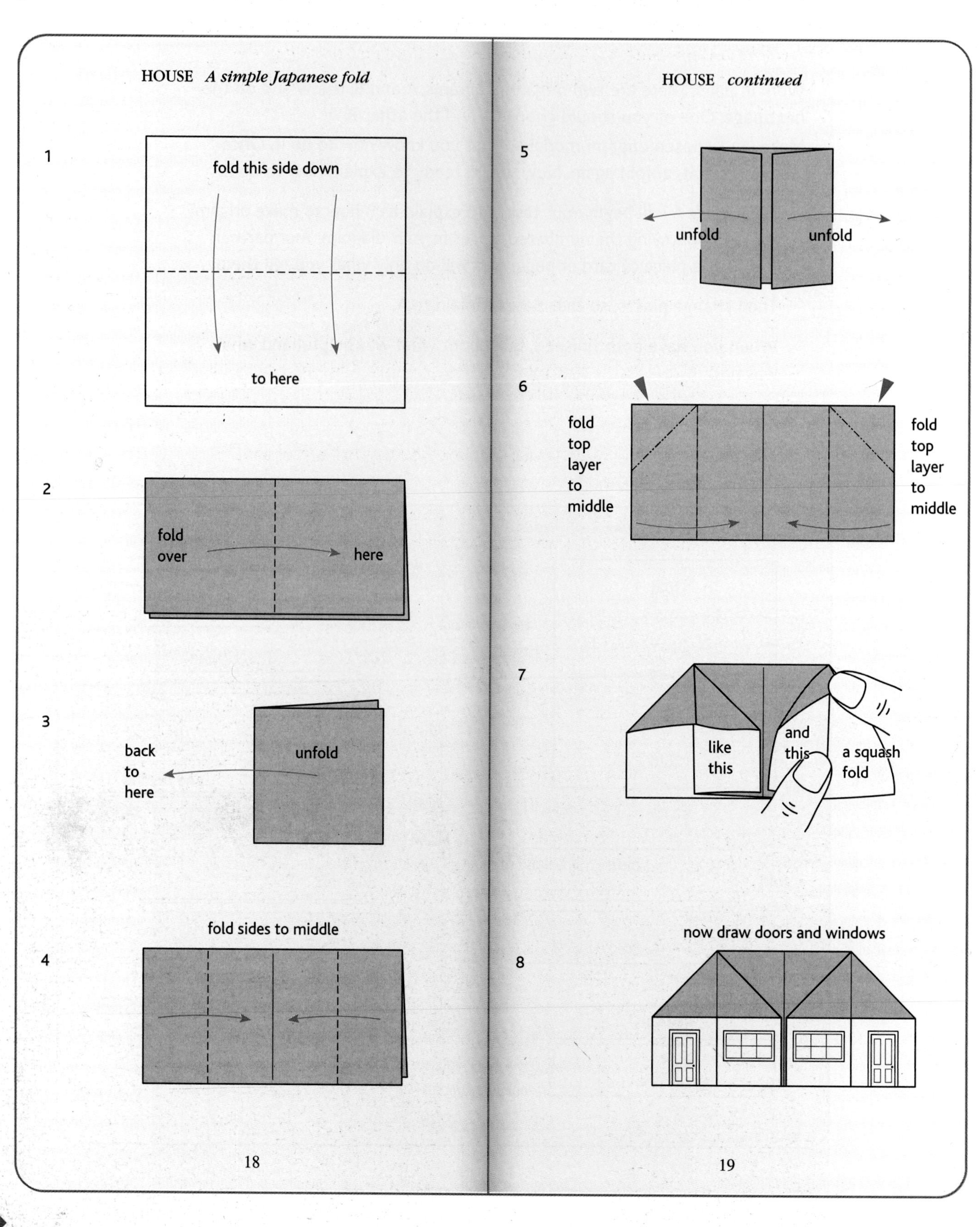
HOUSE A simple Japanese fold
1
fold this side down
to here
2
fold over
here
3
back to here
unfold
4
fold sides to middle
18
HOUSE continued
5
unfold
unfold
6
fold top layer to middle
fold top layer to middle
7
like this
and this
a squash fold
8
now draw doors and windows
19

'Explain yourself!' is usually a kind of threat. It tends to mean someone is in trouble and is going to have to come up with some kind of excuse or explanation that will help the listener understand something they find troubling. This explanation of behaviour or feelings is more 'dramatic' than, for example, giving instructions.

Activity 3 ICT

Working in pairs, improvise a scene. One of you plays a parent or teacher and the other a young person.

Choose one of the following and improvise the scene that might follow. In each case the opening line is spoken by the parent or teacher. The focus of your improvisation should be the explanation of the young person and the parent/teacher's explanation of how they feel.

a It is nine o'clock. You told your mum/dad you would be in at eight. S/he's worried sick.

b You were meant to be in detention. You didn't go. It's the following morning, and the teacher wants to know what happened.

Assignment 5

Plan a presentation to the class on the subject of 'Love and Hate'.

Your talk should be divided into two equal parts. Half will be about things you hate and the other half about things you love. In total it should last no longer than three minutes.

Begin: 'I'll tell you what I hate ...' or 'I'll tell you what I love ...'

The talk is an opportunity for you to describe the things you love and hate, explain why you feel that way, and tell anecdotes to help bring your talk to life.

Preparation

Begin by thinking about, and listing, things you hate and love. Try to have some variety in your list – some serious things and some light-hearted ones.

Once you have decided on a list, think about how much to say about each thing. You probably won't be able to use all of them – there isn't time. There might be one in particular that you know will take up quite a lot of time. Perhaps you'll have quite strong feelings about a couple of things and you may decide to talk about those in detail.

On the other hand, you might prefer to mention a lot of things briefly. It's up to you.

Audience and purpose

Your audience is the class and your teacher. The purpose is to give a talk that will interest and/or entertain them. You might decide that some humour would be a good idea. Everyone in your class will be giving a similar talk, so it's important to try to be a little bit 'different'.

Getting ready

You will probably need some prompt cards. Don't write out a complete script – it's meant to be a talk, not a reading.

What makes a good talk

Your audience would say that if they are interested – if you are interesting – then it's a good talk.

A good talk:

- is organised – it doesn't ramble
- has some variety of tone
- is clear and easy to listen to.

Section D ◆ Language in action
Introduction

In the following units you will learn how language works and how to make language work for you. Understanding how language works will help to improve your skills in speaking and listening, reading and writing.

You will be learning about:

- words, what we call them and their places in sentences
- different types of sentences and how they work
- how sentences are built up
- how sentences fit together in paragraphs
- how to punctuate
- how to spell.

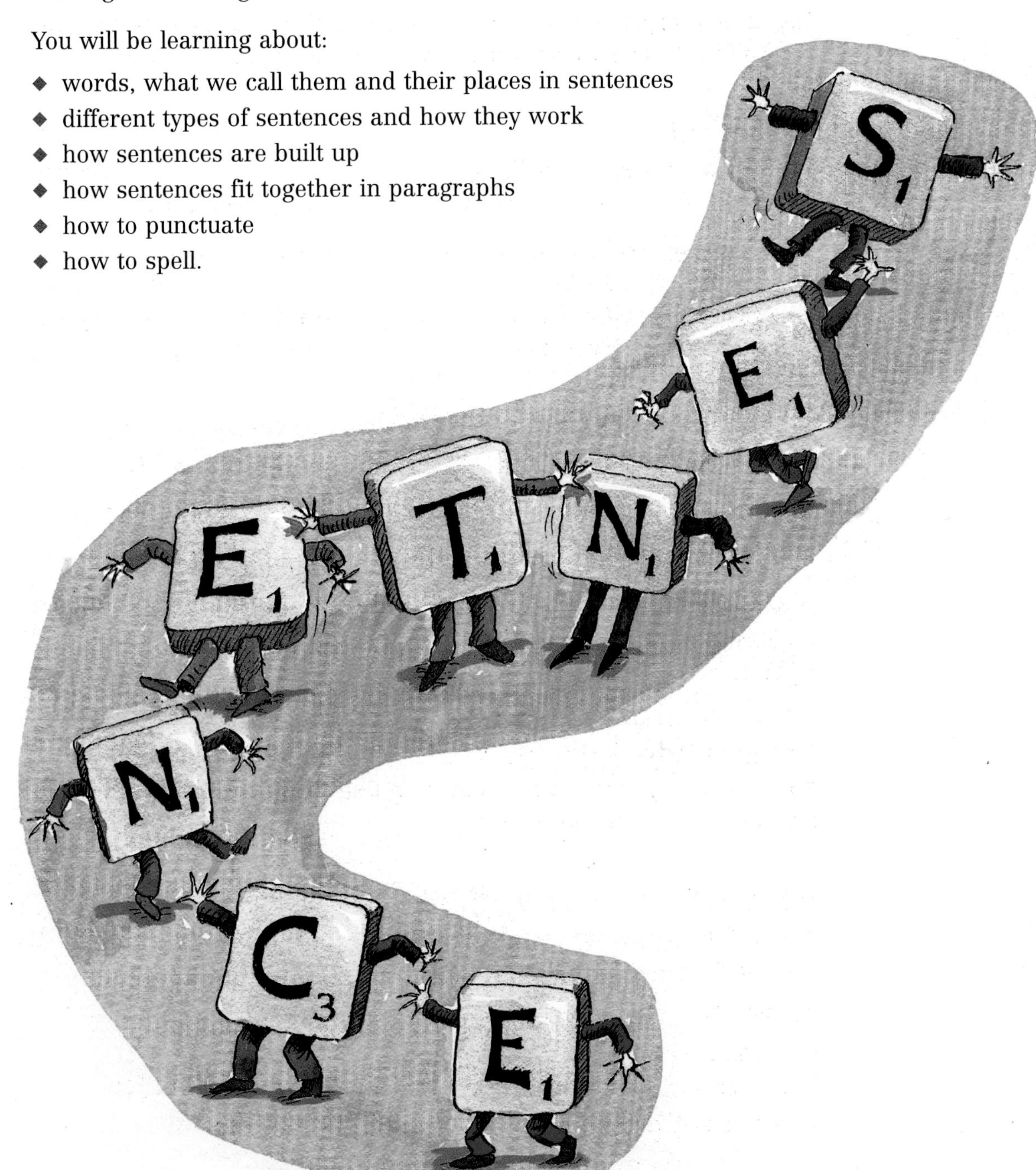

21 Words

This unit will help you to:
- **understand the different jobs that words do**
- **learn how words fit together in sentences.**

There are different kinds of words which do different jobs. It is useful to know what to call these different kinds of words and to understand how they fit together in sentences. This will help you to talk or write about the language used by other writers. This will also help your own writing.

In this unit you will learn about nouns, pronouns, adjectives, verbs and adverbs. All of these are often called parts of speech.

Nouns

We use nouns to name people, places, things, activities or states.
There are several different types of noun:

Proper nouns are always written with a capital letter. They are the names of:

- a particular person (Robbie Williams, Richard Branson)
- a particular place (London, Scotland, Prince's Street)
- a particular book, film or TV show (Goosebumps, Star Wars, Live and Kicking).

Common nouns tell you the name of:

- a person (man, child, woman, driver, stuntman, cyclist)
- an object (bike, computer, video recorder)
- a place (town, village, country, mountain, garden, river)
- an activity (skating, tennis, shopping, cycling, surfing)
- a state (happiness, joy, anger, worry)

You can put one of the following words in front of a common noun: *a an some*.

At the party we had a hamburger and an ice cream each.

Then we listened to some music.

Activity 1 ICT

Read the following extract and write the nouns down in two columns, one headed Proper nouns and one headed Common nouns. Make a chart like the one below.

> Twelve witnesses reported that they saw a bright fireball in the sky last night over Twilton. Rob Gray, a farmer saw the fireball stay in the air for two minutes. Then it disappeared over the hill.
>
> Mr Thompson, from Strange Sightings, was there with a crew of TV cameramen. There will be a report on his programme tonight.

Proper nouns	Common nouns
Twilton	witnesses

You use nouns to name people, places or things, so sometimes writers can use pictures instead of nouns. Look at the example below:

Billy is a little . He lives in a big  with his

Billy has a pet  called Gnasher and a  called Creeps.

Activity 2 WS

Write a story in ten sentences. You may want to use some of the nouns from the list below, or you may want to choose your own. When you have finished, write the story again, using pictures instead of nouns.

- light
- spaceship
- gift
- moon
- alien
- desk
- bedroom.

Pronouns

Nouns are very important because you use them to name things. But sometimes you can use the same noun too often.

Read the example below:

James stepped off the boat feeling very excited. James was about to meet Dr Robinson who was the leader of the expedition. James had always dreamed about travelling to unknown places ...

The writer has repeated the name James several times, and this makes the passage awkward to read. You could replace some of the uses of James with a pronoun. In this case the pronoun would be *he*.

James stepped off the boat feeling very excited. He was about to meet Dr Robinson who was the leader of the expedition.

Pronouns are used to replace the names of people, animals and things. Pronouns can be singular or plural.

Here is a list of pronouns:

Singular			Plural		
I	you	he/she/it	we	you	they
me	you	him/her/it	us	you	them

Activity 1 ICT

Read the following text. Make a list of all the pronouns you can find.

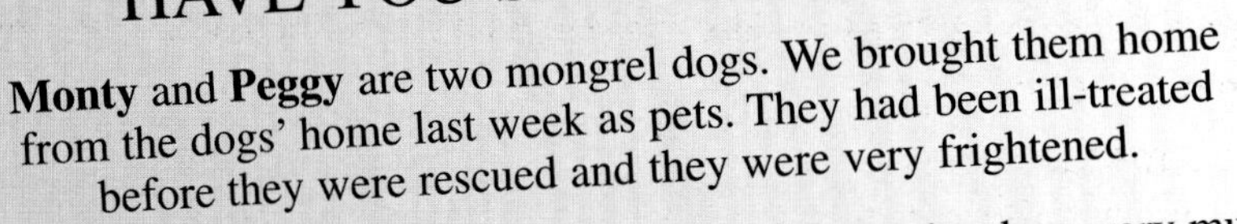

HAVE YOU SEEN TWO DOGS?

Monty and **Peggy** are two mongrel dogs. We brought them home from the dogs' home last week as pets. They had been ill-treated before they were rescued and they were very frightened.

Two days ago they escaped through the hedge. We miss them very much.

Monty is larger than Peggy. He has a smooth brown coat and a black patch over one eye. Peggy is a small dog. She has a white curly coat and a short tail.

If you see them please telephone 954 2162 without delay!

Adjectives

Adjectives are words which add information to nouns.
You can put adjectives before the noun. For example:

	Adjective	Noun		Adjective	Noun
an	expensive	bike	a	happy	baby
a	beautiful	painting	a	massive	pizza

You can also put most adjectives after the words *is*, *are*, *was*, *were*, *feels* or *becomes*.

e.g. He is handsome
They felt fit after their walk.

Activity 1

1 Read the following extract, which Sophie (aged 11) wrote about her mother:

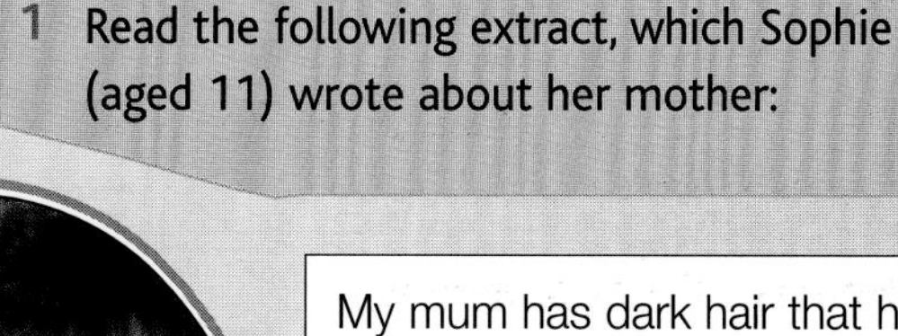

My mum has dark hair that has a life of its own. It bounds across her head like rolling country hills. She has brown glassy eyes encased in her favourite brown and plum make-up.

She has a small round nose and full big lips. She has a lovely face but it's what is on the inside behind that beautiful complexion that counts.

2 Make a list of the adjectives used in this extract.

You will notice that the writer has used several adjectives together in some places.

You can also use adjectives to describe personality and behaviour, as well as appearances, for example:

Sophie's mother is kind.
The naughty child ran into the road.

Activity 2

Choose a member of your own family or a friend and write a short description of them. Use as many adjectives as you can.

1 First make some notes under the following headings:

Name | **Personality**
Appearance *e.g. Face, Hair, Eyes* | **Behaviour**

2 Now write your description and underline the adjectives.

Verbs

Verbs tell us what a person, animal or thing is:

- doing e.g. Bob ran all the way home
- thinking e.g. He wondered what would happen there
- feeling e.g. He worried about his father.

There are also 'being' and 'having' verbs.

to be	to have	to be	to have
I am early	I have a mobile phone	We are early	We have a mobile phone
You are early	You have a mobile phone	You are early	You have a mobile phone
He is early	He has a mobile phone	They are early	They have a mobile phone
She is early	She has a mobile phone		
It is early	It has a mobile phone		

Activity 1 WS ICT

1 Read the following extract and make a list of all the verbs you can find. The first one has been done for you.

The Venus Flytrap catches insects. The insects fly into the plant. Then the plant snaps shut. The insect struggles. The leaves press together. Then the leaves close. The plant dissolves its victim.

2 Read the following passage where some of the verbs have been left out. Choose suitable verbs from the list in the box to complete the passage. You can decide to make Santash and Michelle like or dislike each other according to your choice of verbs.

Santash ________________ across the room. He ________________ Michelle's eye and ________________ at her. He ________________ her a lot. Michelle ________________ back. Does she ________________ the same?

Santash ________________ (towards/away from) her. Michelle ________________ (towards/away from) him '________________ (here/away), Michelle,' he ________________.

catches dislikes stares feel smiles frowns likes glances calls waves shouts moves turns come go

3 Compare your version with a partner's. Has he or she chosen the same words? What difference does it make?

Person

Look at the list below. What do you notice about the endings of the verb?

	Singular	Plural
1st person	I run	we run
2nd person	you run	you run
3rd person	he/she/it runs	they run

The ending of a verb changes according to who is doing the action. We add *–s* to the verb when it is used in the third person singular (with *he*, *she* or *it*).

Some verbs change completely in the third person. An example of this is the verb *to be*:

	Singular	Plural
1st person	I am	we are
2nd person	you are	you are
3rd person	he/she/it is	they are

Activity 1 WS ICT

Write out the following passage using the correct form of the verbs in brackets. The first two have been done for you.

Young Gary Evans (be) is on top of the world. Just 16 years old, he (be) is in the country's greatest football tournament.

'It (be) fantastic,' (state) Gary from his home in a small village near Liverpool. 'My dad (feel) so proud. I (be) nervous, but when I (get) on the pitch, I usually (forget) everything.'

The village (look) very festive as people (prepare) for the big day. There (be) banners saying, 'Well done Gary! We (be) right behind you!'

Activity 2

Look at the sentences below. They have been written by a robot who does not quite understand how our language works. Write out the correct version.

I plays with my friend in the park. He sit on a swing and I goes on the slide. We has a good time. We stays there until five o'clock. Then it am time for tea. My friend come home with me. We eats our favourite meal, pizza and chips followed by ice cream. Then we watches TV until my friend have to go home.

Tenses

Actions can happen in the present (happening now), in the past (has already happened), or in the future (is going to happen). You can use different tenses of a verb to show when an action takes place.

The present tense

You use the *simple present tense* for things we do regularly or all the time:

I swim in the river most days.
We always go to Alton Towers on my birthday.

You also use the simple present tense for statements which are true at the moment, or which are facts that cannot be changed:

African elephants are the world's largest land animals.
They weigh up to 6.5 tons.

There is also another form of the present tense.
This is called the *present continous tense* because you use it to describe things which are happening now:

I am playing a computer game at the moment.
We are watching Eastenders.

You make the present continous tense using the verb *to be* and the -ing form of the main verb.

Activity 1 WS

Write a list of fantastic facts about yourself, using both forms of the present tense. Use the following title:

You Wouldn't Believe Me If I Told You!

The past tense

You use the past tense to talk about actions which are now completed, for example: I swam in the river.

To show that something happened in the past, you can add the suffix *–ed* to some verbs.

I play tennis on Mondays.	present tense
I play**ed** tennis last week.	past tense
He walks to school because he lives nearby.	present tense
He walk**ed** to school because he liv**ed** nearby.	past tense

If the verb already ends in *–e*, you make the past tense by adding *–d*, for example: dive / dived

Read the following extract from *Skellig*. Michael has brought the strange creature he has discovered in the garage some Chinese food. The extract is written in the past tense.

I squeezed between the tea chests. I squatted down beside him. I held the tray up and shone the torch on to the food. He dipped his finger in. He licked his finger and groaned. He stuck his finger in again and hooked a long slimy string of beansprouts and sauce. He stuck his tongue out and licked. He slurped out pieces of pork and mushroom. He shoved the spring rolls into his mouth. The red sauce trickled down from his lips, down over his chin on to his black jacket.

*from **Skellig** by David Almond*

Activity 1

1. Find all the verbs in the past tense and write them down.
2. Which of the verbs describe something the creature did? What impression of the creature do these verbs give you?

Some verbs in English change their shape in the past tense. These are known as strong verbs, for example:

I swim in the river.	present tense
I swam there last year.	past tense
I buy chips for my lunch.	present tense
I bought a takeaway last night.	past tense

Activity 2

Read the passage from *Skellig* again. Which of the verbs are strong verbs? Make a list of them and write down the form of the verb in the present tense.

Activity 3

Fill in the missing letters in the list of strong verbs below.
There are missing letters to fill in from both the present and past tenses of the verb.

Present	Past	Present	Past
think	thought	w - n	w - n
eat	ate	sp - n	sp - n
cat - h	ca - ght	bit -	b - t
fl - ng	fl - ng	tea - -	tau - - t
sw - - g	sw - ng		

You can use two different forms of the past tense:

- You can use the *simple past* form of the verb:
  I played tennis last Saturday.
- You can use the *past continuous* form of the verb:
  I was playing tennis when I sprained my ankle.

This is called the past continuous because it describes actions which continued for some time until they were either completed or interrupted by something else.

Activity 4 WS

Fill in the gaps in these sentences, using the correct tense of the verb in brackets.

When I ________________ (open) the door my friend ________________ ________________ (stand) there. 'Please help me,' she ________(say). I ___________ ______________ (cycle) along the road when the chain on my bike ________________ (break) suddenly. I ________________(fall) off my bike and ________________ (hurt) my leg.

Activity 5 WS

Select an incident from your childhood and write an account of it, using the past tense. You could use one of the suggestions below or think of your own.

- My first day at school
- The surprise
- The quarrel
- The day I got into trouble

The future tense

There are several ways of talking about the future.

You can use the *simple present* tense to talk about fixed arrangements in the very near future:

I am at home all day tomorrow.
I fly to Rome on Monday.

You can use the *present continuous* tense to talk about any fixed future arrangements:

I am going to the cinema this evening.
I am moving to France next summer.

These verb tenses cannot be used to talk about future events which are not fixed. For example, you can say:

My brother is taking GCSE English this summer…
But you cannot say:
…and he is passing it easily.

You can also use *going to* with the verb to talk about the future:

As soon as I leave home, I am going to get a dog.
Are you going to go to the gym this evening?

Finally, you can talk about the future using *shall* or *will*:

I shall finish the job tomorrow.
We will meet them at the airport when their flight gets in.

Activity 1 WS

1. Read this example of a horoscope. Underline all the verbs in the future tense.

Your schoolwork will go well this week, if you put the effort in. An outing with your friends at the weekend will be much more fun than you thought. A sporting success will give your mum reason to be proud of you.

2. Now write a horoscope for your friend. Remember that you are predicting what will happen to your friend, so you will have to write in the future tense.

Adverbs

Adverbs add information to verbs. They tell you *how*, *when* or *where* an action happens.

The giant moved **menacingly** towards Jack. ('menacingly' describes how the giant moved – it is an adverb of manner.)

Then he growled. ('Then' tells us when he growled – it is an adverb of time.)

He threw Jack **outside**. ('outside' describes where Jack was thrown – it is an adverb of place.)

Adverbs of manner

Adverbs can help you to make your writing more vivid and precise and therefore more interesting. Many adverbs of manner end in *–ly*, for example: *quietly*, *fiercely*, *greedily*.

Activity 1

1 Look at the sentences below. Pick out the six adverbs of manner.

Mary walked shakily. Her breath came quickly and she felt a pain stab sharply in her arm. She would not let that happen again. She would speak politely but firmly. She would not let Patsy talk to her rudely and she would not let her push and shove. It was time things changed.

2 What do the adverbs tell us about Mary and how she was feeling?

3 Write a short paragraph of about eight to ten lines following on from this passage, using adverbs of manner to show what the characters are doing and feeling. Underline the adverbs you have used.

Adverbs of time

Adverbs of time tell you about when actions have taken place or when they will take place:

They will arrive *tomorrow*.

Adverbial phrases

Adverbs which are made up of more than one word are called adverbial phrases, for example, *last week*, *three days later*.

On Thursday, I am going on holiday.
We went to Spain *last year*.

Activity 2 ICT

1 Read the following extract and write down the adverbs of time.

Yesterday a series of earth tremors hit the village of Wetherstone. Early in the morning residents were woken suddenly by the sound of breaking glass and crockery falling from shelves. More tremors hit the village again later in the day.

2 Now write a few lines about an incident affecting a town. You could describe a natural disaster, a special event such as a carnival or think of your own situation. Use as many of the adverbs below as you can:

- last week
- recently
- later
- occasionally
- now
- next week.

You can start with the following sentence or think of your own:

Last week, the rain fell. It fell and fell and two days later the floods … .

Adverbs of place

Adverbs can also give you information about where things happen. These are known as adverbs of place.

There is the man you want.
He has been here.
We looked everywhere for him.

Activity 3 ICT

1 Read the following text and write down the three adverbs of place.

The Bluebell Hotel

The Bluebell Family Hotel welcomes families with children of all ages. Here you can be sure to find activities to suit every member of the family. Try out our newly built swimming pool, which has a range of water activities. Nearby you will find our very well equipped gym. Outside, younger children will enjoy the adventure playground with its tree top walk.

2 Use the following adverbs of place in sentences of your own to describe a place you have been to recently, or to describe the picture above:

◆ everywhere ◆ here ◆ nearby ◆ there.

22 Sentences

This unit will help you to:
- **organise your writing into sentences**
- **vary the types of sentence you use to make your writing more interesting.**

A sentence is a group of words that makes complete sense. Sentences begin with a capital letter and end with one of the following:

- a full stop .
- a question mark ?
- an exclamation mark !

Types of sentence

There are four different types of sentence:

Statement

Statements are the most common type of sentence.
The cat ate the mouse.

Question

Questions always ask something.
Did the cat really eat the mouse?

Directive

Directives tell someone to do something.
Don't do that.
Leave that mouse alone.

Exclamation

Exclamations say something surprising, exciting, urgent or awful.
What a terrible mess!

Activity 1 ICT

Make your own collection of directives for display in your classroom. Think carefully about the way directives are used in everyday language. You can find examples of directives when:

- you read junk mail which is delivered to your house, e.g. *Reply today!*
- you read signs in places such as swimming pools or parks, e.g. *Keep off the grass.*
- someone is telling you to do something, e.g. *Tidy your bedroom at once!*

Activity 2

Look closely at the cartoon below, which has been printed without the exclamation marks. Make a list of all the words and sentences which you think should have an exclamation mark.

Activity 3 WS

Look at the list below. Write a question for each situation.

- policeman questioning a suspect car thief
- hairdresser asking a customer about a new hairstyle
- teacher finding out why a pupil was being naughty
- mother speaking to her small child
- football referee speaking to a linesman

Don't forget to use question marks!

Simple sentences

A simple sentence contains one clause only.

A clause has a subject and a verb.

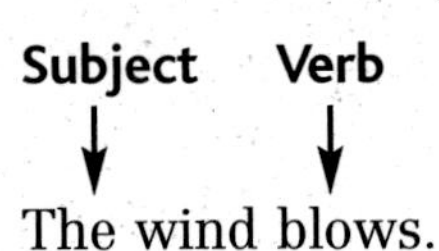

The wind blows.

Anything which comes after the verb in a clause is called the complement.

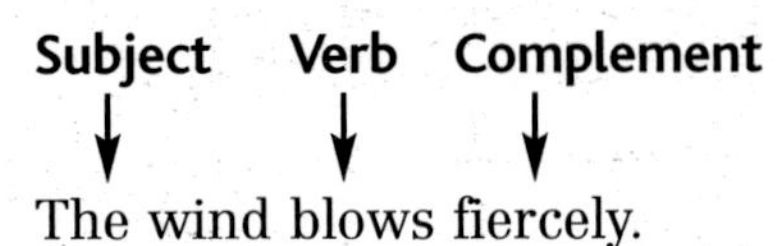

The wind blows fiercely.

Activity 1

Use the word wheel below to make up simple sentences of your own. As long as you have a subject, one complete verb and a complement, you can make any sentence you like.

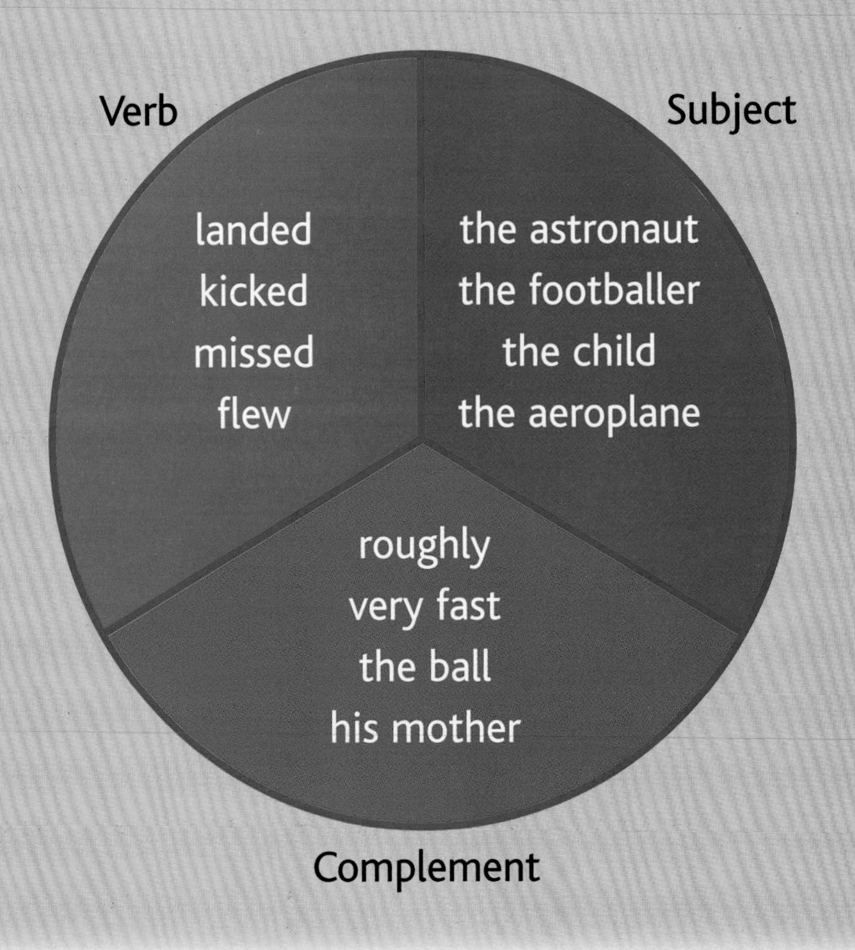

Compound sentences

A connective is a word which links different parts of a sentence. You often use sentences with more than one clause. When you join clauses together with the connectives *and*, *but* or *or*, you make a compound sentence.

I like ice-cream. My friend likes milk-shakes.

I like ice-cream and my friend likes milk-shakes.

In a compound sentence, all the clauses are equally important.

Activity 1 ICT

Read the following extract. Then copy it into your exercise book. Underline all the simple sentences with a straight line. Then underline all the compound sentences with a wiggly line.

The dog is in trouble. It knocked the postman off his bike and it messed up all the letters. The postman was very cross. The dog got caught in the postman's bike and now it has hurt its leg. We took it to the vet. She put a bandage on its leg, but it can't walk very well. We have to stop the dog from going out into the garden. It will not chase the postman for a long, long time.

Complex sentences

You can join clauses together in other ways to show that one clause is more important than another. These sentences are called complex sentences.

Complex sentences consist of a main clause and a subordinate clause. The subordinate clause gives more information about the main clause.

main clause ↓ The old man lived in the farmhouse,

subordinate clause ↓ which was right at the top of the hill.

↑ **connective** (which)

The main clause can make sense on its own. The subordinate clause is linked to the main clause by a connective, such as:

because, although, which, as, where, if, before, after, who.

Activity 1 ICT

1 Read the following extract from a newspaper article about the model dragon which is used during Chinese New Year celebrations.

GEORGE CHAN regularly has to repair the dragon's bamboo framework which can snap easily. This year he also has to mend the pole which holds up the dragon's tail. The pole snapped when the Chinese celebrated the last New Year. His company trains people who want to learn the dragon dance. It is very difficult because they dance the dragon for a long time.

2 Write down the connectives in the extract.

3 Now write down the subordinate clauses which follow each connective.

Activity 2 WS

You need to work with a partner or perhaps a small group for this activity. Together you're going to write a story which uses all of the connectives below (you can change the order if you wish).

You should begin your story with this sentence:

They waited until it was dark ...

After the first sentence you and your partner should take it in turns to write a sentence each. You should aim to write a sentence which uses one of the connectives below.

You can use each connective only once.

- unless
- after
- when
- as if
- until
- so that
- where
- if
- because
- who
- which
- although

23 Paragraphs

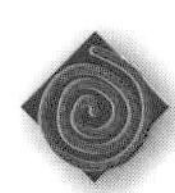

This unit will help you to:
- **group sentences together to form paragraphs**
- **use a topic sentence to begin a paragraph**
- **use words to link paragraphs together.**

You usually group sentences that are about the same topic together in a paragraph. Grouping sentences together and linking them is a very important skill to develop because it helps your readers to make sense of what you have written.

Using paragraphs also divides your work into sections and so makes it easier for readers to read. Paragraphs avoid having one big block of writing on the page, which could be off-putting to a reader. Readers rest during a paragraph break and think about what they have just read.

If you use paragraphs well, you can guide readers through your text. You can show them when you are:

- changing time
- changing place
- changing person or speaker.

Read the extract below, which is taken from a piece of writing about insects. The paragraphs have been taken out of it.

The Natural History Museum has just unveiled its latest amazing exhibition, Creepy Crawlies. As its name suggests, the gallery is dedicated to the lives of insects, spiders and other scuttling creatures. At the museum you can see a real-life ant colony at work. Insect expert Dr Rory
5 Post explained that ants are very social creatures and that they co-operate very well with each other in their ant colonies. In the film *A Bug's Life*, the ants are bullied by a group of nasty grasshoppers. Rory pointed out that this wouldn't actually happen in the natural world because in real life it's the other way round! Ants actually gang up on grasshoppers and bite
10 them. If being bitten by ants isn't enough, grasshoppers can also fall prey to a species of fly whose young bury themselves in the grasshopper's abdomen. The larvae grow and, when they're ready to hatch, burst from the stomach of the grasshopper, killing it in the process.
15 Dr Post told us that not all insects are repellent. He added that most people like butterflies because they look nice and they don't tend to come into the house.

Activity 1

When you have read the text once, see if you can sort it out into paragraphs. There are four paragraphs in this text, each of them dealing with a different topic:

1 general information about the new exhibition at the Museum of Natural History
2 information about ants
3 details of the film *A Bug's Life*
4 information about grasshoppers and other insects.

Rewrite the passage, using appropriate paragraph breaks.

Remember the rule: Sentences on the same topic are placed in the same paragraph. You can get an idea of when a new paragraph begins by looking out for a mention of the new topic in the first sentence of a new paragraph. Look out for a sentence which refers to each of the topics above.

Writers sometimes give the reader clues when they change paragraphs. These clues can be very obvious, words such as *firstly*, *next* and *then*. The clues can also be dates and figures, as in the extract below about the life of the painter, Monet. The paragraphs in this extract have been mixed up but, by using the dates as a guide, you should find it easy to put them in the correct order.

At 19, Monet went to study in Paris where he later worked with Pissarro and Renoir.
By 1900 Monet was regarded as France's leading landscape painter. He was 60 and finally had enough money to live well. He owned a house at Giverny where he built his famous water garden.
Monet was born in Paris in 1840. His father was a grocer and when the family fell on hard times they moved to Sainte-Adresse near the port of Le Havre in Normandy.

Activity 2

Interview a friend about their life and then write down your findings. Organise your writing into three paragraphs on the following topics:

1 date of birth and details about early childhood up to the age of four
2 primary school details
3 arrival at secondary school.

Remember: Your topic sentence tells the reader what the paragraph will be about.

Use dates and ages to help the reader understand the order of events.

Use words such as *next* and *then* to guide the reader through your account.

Using punctuation

This unit will help you to:

- **revise the use of capital letters, full stops, commas, question marks, exclamation marks and punctuation for writing speech**
- **understand how using the right punctuation can help you to explain yourself more clearly and help your readers to appreciate your meaning more easily.**

Punctuation marks

Punctuation is the name for the series of symbols and marks that you use when you are writing to make your meaning clear to your readers. If you did not use capital letters, full stops, commas, question marks and exclamation marks, it would be difficult for your readers to understand exactly what you mean.

When you are speaking you can alter your tone of voice to show whether you are angry or whether you are asking a question. If you are telling a story you can pause at suitable moments to break up your ideas. In writing, of course, none of these things is possible. This is why you need to use punctuation.

Full stops [.]

These are very important punctuation marks because they divide up your writing so that your readers can take in all of your ideas in easy stages. A full stop is used at the end of a sentence, for example: Camilla likes skateboarding.

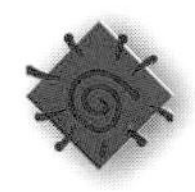

Activity 1 ICT

Read the following extract from *The Growing Pains of Adrian Mole* by Sue Townsend. The full stops have been removed:

I am tired out by the time I have walked a whole mile to school in the morning My father said he used to walk four miles to school and four miles back through wind, rain, snow, hail and broiling sun and fog

There are two sentences here, one where Adrian Mole writes about what he does and one where he writes about his father. The sentences need to be separated by a full stop. Rewrite the extract, putting in the full stops. (Don't forget the one at the end!)

Capital letters

Capital letters are used for several purposes:

- at the beginning of a sentence:
  e.g. My best friend went to the cinema last night.
- for the personal pronoun I:
  e.g. When I get home I listen to music.
- for the first letter of proper nouns, that is, for people's and place's names:
  e.g. Adrian Mole and London
- for days of the week and months of the year e.g. Tuesday, February.

Activity 2

Correct this extract from *My Year* by putting in the capital letters:

january, i now remember, was the month when i had my first office job in london at the age of eighteen. the pay was five pounds a week and i used to travel by train from where we lived in kent to a station in the city of london called cannon street.

Question marks ?

Try asking a friend a few questions and listen carefully to the end of the question. In most questions your voice rises at the end. In writing this is indicated by a question mark, for example, Are you OK?

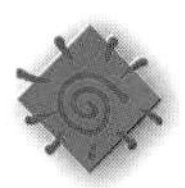

Activity 3 ICT

Ask questions to try to get the answers below. The first one has been done for you.

1 I am going to London. *Where are you going?*
2 I am leaving at eight o'clock in the morning.
3 I am going by train.

Exclamation marks !

Exclamation marks are very useful punctuation marks for indicating that someone is surprised or angry or giving a warning. For example:

◆ Come here! ◆ Look out! ◆ They've won first prize!

Activity 4 ICT

Which of the following needs an exclamation mark?

1 Help
2 Jim is coming too
3 Get out
4 How are you

Commas ,

You use commas to indicate pauses in a piece of writing. They are very important because they help to split a sentence into smaller parts and so they make it easier to read.
You can use them:

- to separate two parts of a sentence:
  As the monster grabbed hold of him, he began to scream very loudly.
- to separate items in a list:
  She would need to take with her for the trip a large rucksack, some strong walking shoes, a waterproof jacket and some warm clothes.

Activity 5 ICT

Correct this extract from *Mrs Frisby and the Rats of Nimh* by Robert C O'Brien by adding commas:
It was a winter house such as some field mice move to when food becomes too scarce and the living too hard in the woods and pastures. In the soft earth of a bean potato pea and asparagus patch there is plenty of food left over for mice after the human crop has been gathered.

Direct speech ' '

Inverted commas, or speech marks, are used to enclose any words that the speaker actually says:

'When can I see you again?' asked James.
'I don't know,' replied Emma softly, looking down at her feet.

Note that you must start a new line each time the speaker changes.

Note also that all the other punctuation – question marks, commas, full stops etc. – appears inside the speech marks.

Activity 6

Punctuate the following passage, using question marks, commas, full stops, speech marks and paragraphing where necessary:
Why do we have to come this way said Jane crossly She hated this part of town There weren't even any decent shop windows to look in Because I want to call in on your grandmother that's why replied her mother briskly Now get a move on and stop moaning

25 Spelling

This unit will help you to improve your spelling by learning spelling strategies.

How well do you spell?

On a scale of 1 to 5, say how far you agree (1) or disagree (5) with the following statements:

- I often make mistakes with easy words.
- If I can't spell a word I make my handwriting untidy so no one will know.
- I've been told I'm too careless with my spelling.
- I'm no good at writing because I can't spell.
- I know I should learn how to spell but I don't know how to.
- I can read lots of words but I can't spell them.
- I get stuck when I try to use a dictionary to check spellings.

If you got mainly 5s, congratulations. You're probably well on the way to being a good speller. Read on and you'll find lots of useful tips to help you improve further.	✓ ✓ ✓ ✓ ✓
If you got mainly 3s, you're starting to gain confidence with your spelling. Read on and by the end of the year you'll be joining the 5s.	✓ ✓ ✓
If you got mainly 1s, then you're almost certainly lacking confidence in your ability to spell. The good news is that a lot of people feel the same way as you do and that you can do something about it.	✓

Very few people think of themselves as good spellers – even though they spell most words correctly most of the time! People often feel bad if they make three or four mistakes in one side of writing. They forget that they got all the other words right. Sometimes lack of confidence in spelling can put them off writing altogether. They won't try out new words, they write as little as possible and even cross out words they have spelled correctly.

Find out how good a speller you really are

Look at the piece of writing by a primary school child on the opposite page. Can you spot the spelling mistakes?

Check with a friend to see if you found the same mistakes.

Be the expert!

What advice would you give this child to help him spell the other words correctly next time?

Write down your suggestions. Try to make them interesting and fun.

Talk about the different ideas you have for helping this child.

my mummy wurcs in an Ofis.
She has her own computa and
a printa and telafon and a
Faxe Mshen. my mummy is
very bisy. She specs to lots
of people on the telafon.
she also rites lots of
impitat leturs. when I am grun
up I want to be a fotballer.
This is becuse I love going
to football with my daddy.

There are many different ways of helping someone to become better at spelling. The first thing you need to understand is that we are all different and we learn things in different ways.

- Some people learn how to spell words by creating a picture of the word in their heads.
- Some find it easier to sound out the word.
- Some need to write out the word to find out if it 'feels' right.

Most often, though, people use a combination of these ways. One of the most popular strategies relies on:

A Seeing the word –
Look at the word. Then shut your eyes and see if you can 'see' it in your head. Do this for at least 10 seconds.

B Sounding the word –
Break the word into different bits and say it slowly, pronouncing each bit separately, e.g. *de – ten – tion*.

C Writing the word –
Cover the word and write it from memory. Try to see it in your head as you write.

Try this out with some words you know you find difficult.

Spelling and handwriting

Researchers have found that there is a clear link between spelling and handwriting. Students often need to write a word to find out if it 'feels' right. This is known as 'muscle memory'. Those who learn to write in a consistent form of joined-up handwriting have a better chance of learning letter patterns this way.

There are two basic movements involved in fluent handwriting:

- the arm moves the hand across the page
- the fingers make the shape of the letters.

Activity 1

1 Make sure your writing arm is supported. (Put your weight on the opposite hand or arm.) Holding your pen, move your arm and hand across the page without moving your fingers.

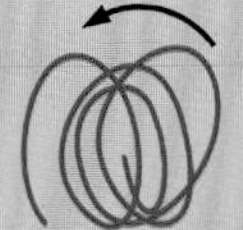
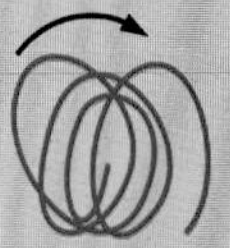

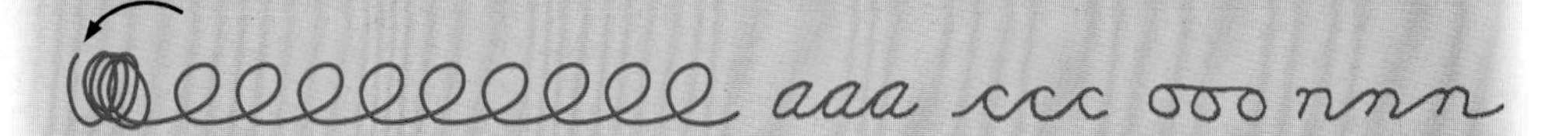

2 Now move your fingers while keeping your hand and arm still.

As soon as you know the correct way to form your letters, your handwriting practice should focus on writing words or common letter combinations e.g. *ight*, *ough*, *ness*, *tion*, *ious*, *ted*. This will help you to build them into your 'muscle memory'.

Handwriting tips

- Don't try to change your handwriting completely – identify one or two things in your own handwriting that you're not happy with and focus on these.
- Experiment with different ways of holding the pen or positioning the paper. Make sure you hold the paper with your non-writing hand.
- You can leave awkward letters unjoined. Don't give up just because you can't join two or three problem letters.
- Frequent short practice sessions are the most useful tips. Aim to spend 5–10 minutes a day on practising your handwriting.
- Write with a fountain pen or a fine fibre-tipped one, not a ballpoint.

Syllables

A syllable is a unit of sound. One useful way of improving your skills in spelling is by breaking words into syllables. By doing this you will learn:

- how words are constructed
- how to remember to spell them.

Look at the way the following words are broken into syllables:

2 syllables		**3 syllables**	
picture	pic + ture	carefully	care + ful + ly
number	num + ber	regular	reg+ u + lar
kitchen	kit + chen	estimate	es + ti + mate

4 syllables

photographic	pho + to + graph + ic
impossible	im + poss + i + ble
introduction	in + tro + duc + tion

Activity 2

In groups, make your own collections of 2-, 3-, and 4-syllable words.
For each word you choose, show where the syllable breaks come.
Can you think of any words with 5 or more syllables? Make a collection of them and show where the syllable breaks come.

Remember:
Improve your chances of spelling a word correctly by breaking it down into syllables.

Activity 3 ICT

Here is a list of the names of some well-known dinosaurs. Break each of the names down into more easily-remembered syllables.

e.g. Dinosaurs: Di + no + saurs

Diplodocus	Compsognathus
Iguanodon	Euplocephalus
Ornithosuchus	Tyrannosaurus
Triceratops	Heterodontosaurus
Protoceratops	Stegosaurus

26 Finding patterns

This unit will help you to spot the patterns that letters make in words so that you will be able to spell them more easily.

Words have patterns. The more word patterns you can recognise, the better your spelling will be. If you group together words which share the same spelling pattern, you are more likely to remember the pattern and learn the words quickly. In time you will automatically use these patterns when you are spelling similar words.

Look at the word groups below and see if you find the pattern for each group. You should find some of these groups easier than others.

sick	measles	interest	vicious	believe
crockery	measure	difference	poisonous	retrieve
quick	feat	desperate	anxious	relieve
jockey	treasure	filter	colour	thief
limerick	reason	deliberate	four	receive
locksmith	real	observe	mouse	deceive
speckled	heavy	baker	humour	conceive*

*There is a spelling rule for words in this column which you may already know.

Activity 1 ICT

Now make up your own sets of words using letters from the following groups:

ee, ll, or, ow, ough.

Use a dictionary to help you.

Many words change their endings according to how they are used in a sentence. Once you have learned the patterns for these changes, you should be able to use them again and again without making mistakes.

Singular and plural

When you talk or write about one person, place, thing, activity or state, you use a singular noun:

We went on an aeroplane to Majorca.

When you talk about more than one person, place, thing, activity or state, you use a plural noun:

When we got there, we hired motorbikes.

To make most nouns plural, add –s:

motorbike ⟶ motorbikes

To make nouns that end in *s*, *x*, *ch*, *sh*, *z*, plural, add *–es*:

fox ⟶ foxes   church ⟶ churches

To make nouns that end in *–y* plural, add *–s* if the letter before *y* is *a*, *e*, *o* or *u*:

tray ⟶ trays   toy ⟶ toys

When letter before *y* is a consonant (any letter that is not *a*, *e*, *o* or *u*) take off the *y* and add *–ies*:

baby ⟶ babies

To make nouns that end in *–ff* plural add an *–s*:

sheriff ⟶ sheriffs   cuff ⟶ cuffs

Some nouns that end in *–f* are made plural by adding an *–s*:

chief ⟶ chiefs   reef ⟶ reefs

Some nouns that end in *–f* or *–fe* are made plural by changing the *–f* or *–fe* to *–ves*:

thief   thieves   knife   knives

Activity 1 ICT

Complete the following passage with nouns from the box below.
You will have to change the nouns from singular to plural.

It is many ________________ ago now; I was a girl of fifteen and I went to visit a small up-county town. It was young in those ________________ , and two days' journey from the nearest village. The population consisted mainly of ________________ . A few were married and had their ________________ and ________________ , but most were single.

day child man wife year

Adding suffixes

Many words are made up of different parts. The main part of a word is called the **stem**. It is often possible to add a **suffix** after the stem to change the meaning of the stem:

e.g.	**stem**	+	**suffix**	
	perform	+	ance	= performance

Activity 1 ICT

Copy out the words in the list below and underline the stem in each case:

1 performance
2 noticeable
3 hopefully
4 triumphant
5 careless
6 guilty
7 experienced
8 courageous
9 kindness
10 listening

Changing verb endings

You have already seen that you can add the suffixes *–ed* or *–d* to the ends of many verbs to make the past tense. There are some other rules for changing the endings of verbs which will help you to spell them correctly.

Adding –ing

With many verbs, you simply add *–ing* to the stem of the verb:

e.g.

push	pushing
lean	leaning

If the verb has one syllable and ends with *–e*,
you remove the *–e* and add *-ing*:

skate	skating	drive	driving
like	liking	make	making

Activity 2

Make a list of ten verbs that end in *–e* and follow this rule.

If the verb has one syllable and a short vowel and ends in a single consonant, you double the consonant and add *–ing*:

e.g. sit sitting
clip clipping

Activity 3

Make a list of ten verbs that follow this rule.

Adding –ed

With many verbs you simply add *–ed* to the stem of the verb:

e.g. push pushed
walk walked

However, if the verb already ends in *–e*, you just add *–d*:

e.g. rake raked
like liked

If the verb has one syllable and a short vowel and ends with a single consonant, you double the consonant and add *–ed*.

e.g. rob robbed
pop popped

Adding –d and –s to verbs that end in –y

If the verb ends with a consonant + *–y*, you change the *–y* to *ie* and add *–s* or *–d*:

e.g. try tries tried
fry fries fried

Activity 4

Add *–ed* to each of the following verbs, making any necessary changes.

1 bang
2 hurry
3 spy
4 supply
5 try
6 haunt
7 empty
8 scrap
9 trip
10 pot

GLOSSARY

archaic a word no longer in ordinary use (see page 21).
audience the people attending, listening to something (see page 60).
contrast a striking difference between two things (see page 37)
couplet two lines of poetry that come together, often rhyming (see page 108).
device used for a particular purpose. (see page 28).
direct speech the exact words spoken by a speaker (see page 127).
drama a play or other script (see page 94).
epic a long story of heroic events and actions (see page 12).
form the shape or structure. Example: the shape of a poem (see page 22).
formal speech speech that follows accepted rules or customs (see page 64).
free verse poetry that has neither rhyme nor regular rhythm (see page 26).
homophone a word with the same sound as another but with a different meaning or spelling. Example read/reed (see page 159).
image a picture created by words which helps the reader to imagine what the writer is describing (see page 30).
informal speech speech without ceremony or formality (see page 64).
internal rhyme the positioning of rhyming words within a line of poetry. Example: 'Though the threat of snow was growing slowly ...' (see page 29).
legend a traditional tale about a person or country, often regarded locally as history, but which may or may not be true (see page 19).
mnemonic a short verse, phrase or other device which helps one to remember. Example: 'there is a rat in separate' (see page 159).
myth a traditional tale, usually about supernatural beings or events, sometimes used as an explanation of natural events (see page 9).
narrator the voice telling the story or poem (see page 18).
paragraph a group of sentences placed together because they have a common idea, beginning on a new line of the page (see page 26).
prefix a group of letters attached to the beginning of a word to form another word. Common prefixes include: 'anti-', 'auto-', 'extra-', 'inter-', 'multi-', 'non-', 're-', 'un-' (see page 159).
prose writing or speech with no formal rhythm or pattern, as distinct from poetry (see page 40).
punctuation marks in written texts to indicate phrases, sentences, possession etc, such as commas, full stops, apostrophes, speech marks (see page 181).
repetition when the same word or phrase is used again (see page 22).
rhyme the repetition of similar or identical sounds. Example: 'park', 'mark' and 'lark' (see page 22).
rhythm the pattern of emphasised sounds in a line (see page 109).
scanning to read quickly in order to find a particular point (see page 68).
setting where and when events take place (see page 39).
simile an image in which the writer compares one thing to another using 'like' or 'as'. Example: 'he chattered like a magpie' (see page 22).
singular expressing only one (see page 189).
skimming to read superficially to understand the general meaning (see page 70).
stanza poems are often organised into groups of lines called stanzas or verses (see page 26).
stem the main part of a word to which prefixes and suffixes are attached (see page 190).
suffix a group of letters attached to the end of a word to form another word. Common suffixes include: '-able', '-ent', '-ese', '-ible', '-ize', '-ish', '-ism', '-ness' (see page 159).
synonym a word with the same or a similar meaning as another (see page 91).
thesaurus a book of words and phrases grouped according to meaning (see page 91).